SMILING AT YOURSELF

SMILING AT YOURSELF

EDUCATING YOUNG CHILDREN
ABOUT STRESS AND SELF-ESTEEM

Allen N. Mendler, PhD

*Suggestions for teachers, parents and other care providers
of children to age 10*

Network Publications, a division of ETR Associates
Santa Cruz, CA
1990

10 9 8 7 6 5 4 3

Printed in the United States of America

Illustrations by Marcia Quackenbush

Library of Congress Cataloging-in-Publication Data

Mendler, Allen N.
    Smiling at yourself : educating young children about stress and self-esteem / Allen N. Mendler.
        p.   cm.
    Includes bibliographic references.
    ISBN 0-941816-90-7
    1. Stress management—Study and teaching (Elementary) 2. Problem-solving—Study and teaching (Elementary) 3. Self-respect—Study and teaching (Elementary)   I. Title.
    RA785.M46   1990
    649'.64—dc20   89-13288
                                                CIP

Title No. 506

For children everywhere, who deserve a childhood in which they learn to love, to give and to smile.

Allen Mendler

Contents

Acknowledgments

I'd like to express my gratitude and appreciation to many people who have encouraged and helped me in the completion of this book.

My dear friend and colleague Rick Curwin gave me valuable content input and was always there to bolster my self-esteem when I needed a booster shot. Martha Bulger offered preliminary illustrations that helped me picture some of the concepts I have tried to convey. Linda Steinberg, Andrea Yekutiel, Wanda Lincoln, Georgia Archibald and my wife Barbara Mendler read the book from the perspective of the teacher and offered valued advice. Dr. Martin Krupnick, my close friend and colleague, offered feedback from the perspective of the clinical psychologist. My sons Jason and Brian used many of these activities first as sort of guinea pigs and helped me modify them along the way. They also gave me many ideas which I converted into strategies and activities. My thanks and love to them. I also want to thank Bob Peterson, Ruby Taylor and staff at the TWIXT program in Rochester, NY; my sibling group; Paul Scott, Gloria Forgione, Drs. Bob Miller and Jim MacWhinney at Mary Cariola Children's Center in Rochester; Frank Pasanello and the staff at United Cerebral Palsy of Rochester; Moe Bickweat, staff and the boys at Oatka Residential Center at Industry, NY; and staff and students in the Webster School District. You have all contributed in numerous ways to my self-esteem and my knowledge base.

A very special thanks to the late Dr. Peg Kintz whose gentle, effective manner of relating to people in a dignified way serves as a model for how we human beings can enrich each other's lives.

Finally, it has been a pleasure to work with Kathleen Middleton and staff at ETR whose input, patience, caring and support has made this project a reality.

Note to the Reader

This book has been designed to provide parents, teachers and care givers both *content and ideas* for practical application of current theory about stress and self-esteem in young children. The content has been presented in a very personal and direct way so that it is easily understood and used. Practical application comes in the form of activities for children. While some children can read for themselves, the activities are designed to be conducted by adults. The author has taken great care in providing directions for the activities in words that he would use in explaining the activity directly to children. It is recommended that parents and teachers use his words as a model for helping children with activities. He also recommends that while the activities are for kids, parents and teachers will benefit too!

Introduction

For Parents and Teachers

Billy is a whirlwind who can't settle down in school. Maria refuses to do her chores around the house and her work at school. Sam cries when his friend doesn't ring the doorbell. Bobby is forever teasing his little sister, Cassandra, leading to fights and tears. Susan is convinced she's too fat, too dumb and too ugly to ever have a boyfriend. Jose is forever promising to mow the lawn but always seems to forget. Jennifer feels unloved but finally has a group of friends. Unfortunately, her friends insist that she do drugs in order to be part of the gang. These behaviors may be symptoms of **stress** and **low self-esteem**.

A recent survey of more than 4,000 Kansas school children in kindergarten through third grade showed that 42% experienced negative stress behavior such as headaches, difficulty sleeping, stomach aches, worries about doing poorly in school, biting fingernails and having short tempers (Associated Press, "Stress is Hurting Kids, Says Study." *Rochester, NY Democrat and Chronicle,* 13 April, 1989*)*.

This data was from a state where the pace of living is not as frantic as in more populated states. Children in these states probably have even higher stress levels. Many studies have found that suicide, an irreversible solution to the problem of stress, is increasing among teenagers and young adults.

This is a book written for children about stress. As a parent or teacher you want your children to be happy and able to cope with the many life events that can be trying. You want your children to achieve well at school, to have friends, to hang out with the *right* crowd, to make good decisions and to solve problems in a way that doesn't do damage either to themselves or others.

You want them to experience life's conflicts as challenges to be met rather than as excuses to fail. You want them to understand that it's okay for them to have a point of view that differs from yours and to express this disagreement in ways that promote integrity rather than disrespect.

We may often forget that while childhood is indeed a time for fun and play, it is also a time of intense stress for many. It is a time of life in which each child struggles to define his own individuality, his own degree of competence and where he stands within the larger family and social context. Most importantly, the child makes key decisions about the kind of person he is that strongly influence what he does and how he is later in life.

Symptoms of stress in children, as with adults, may take many different forms. Some of the more common behaviors associated with stress are: underachievement at school, depression, irritability, anxiety, fatigue, nightmares, hyperactivity, aggressive behavior, withdrawal from others, nervous laughter, body aches and emotional tension. All children experience symptoms of stress some of the time.

Those with low self-esteem are especially vulnerable to developing stress disorders. As parents and teachers it is our responsibility to help our children see themselves positively so that they'll know how to cope with stressful events that come their way.

This book is written to assist children in understanding what stress is and what they can do about it. It defines stress as unpleasant feelings associated with events that range from being teased by a bully on the bus to feeling unloved by important people in their lives.

Self-esteem is defined as the beliefs and attitudes that we have about ourselves; the self-judgments we make regarding our skills and abilities. I'm worthwhile, good, bad, a loser, a winner, smart, stupid, clumsy, well-coordinated are but a few of many value judgments we make that influence our over-all self-concept. The more positive our judgments—the higher our self-esteem.

The book includes several *problem-solving* methods that assist with the challenges of teaching children to like themselves, how to feel in charge of things that happen to them, to take responsibility for decisions they make and how to effectively solve problems with other people.

The *relaxation* methods show children how to safely release their angry feelings and how to make themselves feel calm even when they are unable to identify what it is that makes them tense.

Some of these methods help when the things that cause stress are acute and clearly definable (i.e., moving to a new neighborhood where you don't know anybody), while others address those that are prolonged and ambiguous (i.e., generally not liking oneself).

My hope is that this book contributes to helping children with current stress-related problems learn how to cope more effectively, as well as providing a guide for ways in which all children can increase their tolerance to difficult life events. Just as a vaccine prevents later disease, so too can effective early practice reduce the likelihood of stress harming a child.

For Kids

- ❦ Stress is when your brother teases you by calling you names. *You feel angry.*
- ❦ Stress is when you're working on an arithmetic problem all morning but you can't get it right. *You feel frustrated.*
- ❦ Stress is when you want something real bad but your mom won't buy it for you. *You feel unloved.*

- Stress is when you break a glass and get yelled at. *You feel worried.*
- Stress is when you try out for a team and you don't make it. *You feel worthless.*
- Stress is when you say the wrong answer in class. *You worry that other kids will laugh.*
- Stress is when other kids start picking on you. *You're afraid you'll get hurt.*
- Stress is when you can't find someone to play with or talk to. *You feel lonely.*
- Stress is when everybody seems to notice only your superstar sister. *You feel jealous.*
- Stress is when your parents fight or get divorced or when one of them dies. *You feel sad and maybe even guilty that it's your fault.*

These are just some of the things that happen to kids that make them feel uptight, annoyed, tense, sad or angry. Stress is another word that is often used when we think about these kinds of feelings.

All kids sometimes feel stress. You may feel torn between what you want to do and what teachers or parents want you to do. There are times when you feel pressured: pressured to achieve, pressured to do what friends want, pressured to fit in and maybe even pressured to take drugs.

Kids who handle stress well are able to find ways to make themselves feel better without hurting either themselves or other people. When they feel worried about school, they quit worrying and start working. When they get laughed at by other kids, they say "everybody makes mistakes sometimes," not "shut up or I'll break your nose!"

They can say no to drugs and other harmful things because they understand that life has its ups and downs. They know that things aren't always going to go smoothly. They mostly like themselves;

when they look in a mirror, they usually like who they see. And when they don't, they can make a plan that helps them do better. They have high *self-esteem.*

Kids who use drugs or alcohol, who mess up in school on purpose, who get into a lot of fights, who feel down in the dumps a lot, who often think that they are dumb, stupid or unlovable, or who do risky, dangerous things to make others care about and notice them have serious problems with stress and self-esteem.

This book can help. You can learn that you are a special, valuable person who deserves to be cared about and loved. If you are already handling stress well, this book will show you even more ways to deal successfully with life's pressures.

If you aren't coping well, this book can help you realize that you have more control over what happens to you than you think. It is never too late to learn how to TAKE CHARGE OF YOUR LIFE!!!

This book is about stress and what you can do about it. It is an activity book that asks you to try lots of different things. You can do each activity alone, or you can have a friend, parent or teacher read the directions to you while you do the activity. You might even want to give the book to a teacher, a guidance counselor or your parents. Then they can help other kids learn how to deal with their problems better.

How to Use This Book

There are five chapters in this book. Chapter 1 helps you learn how to like yourself better by learning to feel proud of yourself, learning to reward yourself and learning how to have power over what happens to you.

Chapter 2 shows you lots of ways to make both your mind and your body feel more calm and relaxed. If you feel angry, if you feel sad, if you worry or if a part of your body feels tight, there are lots of easy ways to feel better. In this chapter you will also discover how you can make relaxing "movies" in your mind that will make you a calmer, happier person.

Chapter 3 shows you lots of things you can do to safely get rid of unpleasant feelings without hurting either yourself or other people.

Chapter 4 provides several activities that teach you how to get along better with other people and especially, how to handle people that make you mad.

Chapter 5 is about big problems that cause stress, such as illness in the family, abuse, the death of a loved one, divorce, drug use and suicide.

Each chapter begins with a section for parents and teachers. An explanation and an overview of the concepts and activities related to these concepts is provided. Most activities include another section called **Parents and Teachers Can...,** which advises how best to help children get the most out of the activity. Ideas for how you can follow up on what a child has learned are included in this section. As such, the book is as much a guide for parents to assist their children as it is a *how-to* book for kids. Teachers will also find the activities applicable to promoting relaxation and positive mental health in the classroom.

Each chapter contains several activities. These are found in sections identified as **Activity for Kids....** Your guidance, wisdom and knowledge of specific children is critical in selecting or adapting the various activities for maximum benefit to each child.

While some children can read for themselves, activities are most effective with you reading the directions while children experience or practice the content. The activities are written so parents and teachers can use the words and directions provided to guide children through activities. You may want to do many of the activities along with children. Most are as effective for adults as they are for children. Unlike Procrustes, the robber of ancient Attica who forced his victims to fit on his iron bed either by trimming their legs or by stretching their bodies, your guidance in selecting activities that best *fit the child* as well as your style of parenting or teaching can be most helpful.

All kids can learn from this book: kids who feel nervous before a test or baseball game, kids who have trouble making friends, kids who can't settle down in school, kids who are feeling unsuccessful, kids who are using or thinking of using drugs, kids who want to become more creative in how they deal with themselves and others.

Directions

1. Read through the book and help children *do the activities.* Just as you can't build a model airplane or ride a bicycle just by reading the directions, you also can't help children like themselves more, get along better with others or feel calm only by reading.

2. Learning to deal with stress takes *time and practice.* Help children with at least one or two activities every day.

3. Help children *keep doing the activities* that are the most useful or that feel the best.

Good luck, and enjoy the process of helping children become happier, calmer and friendlier.

Chapter 1

Liking Yourself

To Parents and Teachers

The activities presented in this chapter are designed to help children learn and enhance the development of positive self-esteem. Feeling good about oneself is the foundation upon which the child builds resources to cope with the stress caused by unpleasant events. The better children feel about themselves, the more capable they are of handling life's frustrations and disappointments.

Children with high self-esteem are open to evaluating the opinions and judgments of others without being dependent upon others for feelings of self-worth. They feel worthwhile because they realize that nobody is approved of or loved by everybody all the time.

They develop an "I can do it" attitude, believing themselves to be in control of and responsible for what happens to them. They can pat themselves on the back when proud of an accomplishment and use non-success as a vehicle for increased future effort.

As a parent or teacher, your guidance in assisting to elevate children's self-esteem is extremely important. You can supplement the activities in this chapter in the following ways:

- ❧ Be specific with a child when you give feedback. Tell the child clearly what he or she did that makes you feel pleased or disappointed.
- ❧ Help children to establish a *plan of action* or guide for success on a given task.
- ❧ Help children learn to attribute non-success to insufficient effort rather than to a lack of ability. Kids can improve when they believe more effort will lead to better outcomes. They don't develop positive self-esteem when the tasks that they are given are too difficult or when they believe themselves to be "too stupid" to succeed.

❦ Help children learn how to reward themselves for accomplishment by working with them to develop identifiable goals and earned privileges for attaining these goals.

❦ Children develop healthy self-esteem by becoming masters of their environment. Teach them mastery by offering lots of opportunities to make choices, guidance in anticipating the probable consequences of each choice (If I do *A* then *B* might happen.), and responsibility in accepting the outcome (I did *A* and *B* happened. I don't like *B*. Next time I'll do *C.*).

❦ Encourage children's developing empathy for others by having them be helpers to those less fortunate. Giving help to others makes kids feel good about themselves.

❦ Be a good role model. Make your own actions like those you expect from children.

To Kids

The activities in this chapter show you how to:

❦ *Feel proud of yourself.*
❦ *Reward yourself for your best effort.*
❦ *Have power over what happens to you.*
❦ *Care about yourself.*
❦ *Love yourself.*

Smiling at Yourself ▪▪▪▪▪▪▪▪▪▪▪▪▪▪▪▪▪▪▪▪▪▪▪▪

For Parents and Teachers...

Some scientists, including Robert Levenson of Indiana University, have found that when you express a negative emotion on your face, even if you don't mean it, your body actually experiences it. Smiling, it is claimed, at least keeps your body's reaction "neutral."

Related research has found that facial expressions are actually a *cause* of emotion, not only what we see as a *result* of emotion. When people are feeling good about themselves, it is as if they are smiling inside.

With young children, we can teach them the power of positive inner feeling when they learn to appreciate themselves by smiling. Next time you are uptight, close your eyes and put a happy smile on your face...Isn't it hard to stay uptight when you do that?...Encourage your children to respond similarly with this activity.

Parents and Teachers Can...

Assist the child in evaluating the effectiveness of this activity. Suggest that feelings be rated before and after doing this activity by using the "Smiling at Yourself Rating Scale" in Appendix A.

Activity for Kids...*

1. Look into the mirror and put a happy smile on your face. It might help for you to think of something funny that has happened in the past that made you smile from your teeth to your toes.

2. Notice yourself smiling into the mirror as you think about this funny thing.

3. Now go to your room or another quiet place where you won't be bothered. Lie down on your bed or sit down in a comfortable spot.

4. Close your eyes and picture in your mind that happy smiling face from the mirror looking at your eyes. Very slowly let that smiling face move itself down to your mouth. Now with your eyes still closed, you'll begin to notice your lips start to smile.

5. Now let the smile work itself all the way through your throat and into your stomach. Notice how your stomach begins to feel tingly as if you want to laugh. Keep looking at that smiling face from the mirror move all the way through your stomach, to your legs, ankles, and toes. You begin to feel sparkly all over your body from the top of your head to the tips of your toes.

6. Keep enjoying this happy feeling...whenever you want, open your eyes and realize how much power you have to make yourself feel happy.

7. The next time you are in a grouchy mood, whether at home, school or at a family visit, try smiling at yourself.

* Adapted with permission from *Discipline with Dignity,* by R. Curwin and A. Mendler. Alexandria, VA: Association for Supervision and Curriculum Development, 1988. Also, in *Effective Discipline: Solving Problems at the Source.* Springhouse, PA: Learning Institute, 1988.

Laughing ■■

For Parents and Teachers and Kids...

Laughing all the way from deep down in your stomach up through your chest and out your mouth is one of the best things you can do to feel good. A man named Norman Cousins wrote a book a few years ago and told about how he cured himself of a serious illness by *laughing,* after doctors had told him that there was nothing they could do to make him better. Mr. Cousins watched a lot of funny movies that made him laugh and made his body heal.

Nobody is suggesting that children or adults watch funny movies all day every day. But children and adults should have a fun time every day. This is a time that you ONLY do things that make you feel terrific. Maybe it is telling jokes with a friend or acting very silly. Maybe it's having a friend tickle you. Maybe it is listening to a funny comedian or watching a funny movie. Maybe it is different things on different days. What are some things you did today that were fun?

Parents and Teachers Can...

Help the child to identify fun times by suggesting specific activities that you know he likes. Some children feel guilty when they have fun because they worry that adults think of them as irresponsible. Your permission and encouragement of fun will enable a child to more fully feel this joy. It's also a good idea for you, the parent and/or teacher, to give yourself a fun time each day (with or without a child). Suggest that your child use the "Fun Rating Scale" (see Appendix A) so that he can experience changes associated with this activity.

Activity for Kids...*

Think about the things you did or enjoyed today that were fun. Make a list. Or, draw a picture of each thing. Mount your list or pictures on a wall to admire.

Questions:

1. Who are some people that make you laugh? You might want to spend some time with them.

2. What is funny to you? What makes you laugh? Do you do a little of this every day?

3. Do you like the idea of having a fun time every day? What might you do?

4. If it is hard for you to think about doing this, maybe you would feel more comfortable picturing funny things in your mind. Picture your mother serving dinner while she is walking on her hands; picture your friend talking as ink runs down the side of her mouth (and she doesn't know it).

Get the idea? Try it—HAVE FUN—you'll enjoy life more!

* Adapted with permission from *Discipline with Dignity,* by R. Curwin and A. Mendler. Alexandria, VA: Association for Supervision and Curriculum Development, 1988. Also, in *Effective Discipline: Solving Problems at the Source.* Springhouse, PA: Learning Institute, 1988.

Appreciate Yourself━━━━━━━━━━━━━━━

For Parents and Teachers...

We have all heard the saying, "the squeaky wheel gets the oil." Because so much goes on in our lives, it is perhaps natural that we mostly notice when things aren't going well and take it for granted when things are. For example, we're more likely to notice and criticize when the toys haven't been picked up than we are to say "thank you" after the child has done as requested.

We're more likely to attend to the fidgety child when she is out of her seat than to notice her when she is seated (even if that's infrequently). We are more likely to feel and express our disappointment at our "bright" child's C than we are to respond to the effort expended by the child that resulted in the grade (especially if it wasn't the *maximum* effort).

We can help our children learn to appreciate themselves by first acknowledging them when they have made an effort and then even more importantly, telling them to give themselves a deserved "pat-on-the-back." We are better able to do this with children when we have first done it for ourselves. Most parents do not get much, if any, appreciation from their kids. When is the last time your child said, "Gee Mom, thanks a lot for driving me all over town. You sure are the best!" For a teacher, how often do kids say, "Boy, that was an interesting, exciting lesson. I learned a lot. Thanks!"

We need to take good emotional care of ourselves through self-acknowledgment and appreciation. By the way, don't hesitate to ask your kids for appreciation. You might say, "I worked really hard to make dinner, and I'd feel good about a thank-you." Kids and adults with high self-esteem are those who have learned to see themselves as competent, capable and worthy of appreciation by others and themselves. You can help children by giving them your appreciation.

Parents and Teachers Can...

Enhance a child's pride of accomplishment by appreciating her efforts. As parents and teachers, we often need reminders to recognize children when they have acted and behaved in positive ways. Thanking your child for making the bed will go much further than criticism for not making it.

When a child is putting forth effort in doing school work, walking the dog (even with a frown on the face) or taking out the trash, these are worthy of your positive comments. Each day, make a point of noticing at least one thing that a child says, does or expresses that you appreciate. Then tell her!

Activity for Kids...

1. Keep a notebook of things you do, say or feel each day that make you feel proud. (See "Notebook of Appreciations" in Appendix A.)

2. Be a helper. Most people feel great about themselves when they do something for somebody else.

- ❦ Help a little kid cross the street
- ❦ Give your seat to an older person on the bus
- ❦ Offer to carry someone's groceries to the car
- ❦ Volunteer to give your time at a school
- ❦ Smile at others and say a friendly hello.

There are lots of ways to help people. Can you think of other ways to be a helper? You might want to write these down. Or, draw a picture.

I can be a helper today by:
   a.
   b.
   c.

3. Take a large sheet of paper and hang it on a wall. Write your name on it and if you want, paste a picture of yourself right in the middle of the page.

4. Whenever you act in a way that was helpful to somebody else and made you feel proud, write down a couple of words about what you did on the paper. You might also ask teachers, family members or friends to write on your chart when they appreciate something that you did.

I helped my little
brother get dressed.
I helped Grandma
cook dinner.

Setting a Goal ▪▪▪▪▪▪▪▪▪▪▪▪▪▪▪▪▪▪▪▪▪▪▪▪▪▪▪▪▪▪▪▪▪▪▪

For Parents and Teachers...

Successful kids and adults are often able to identify their goals and then take the necessary steps to reach them. When difficulties occur they may feel frustrated or upset, but having a goal enables them to keep a "picture" in their minds of what they are aiming for.

These kids can tolerate occasional setbacks because they understand that achievement requires effort and is often difficult. This activity helps show you how to assist youngsters in understanding what goals are and how to go about meeting them.

Parents and Teachers Can...

Help children enjoy setting goals (e.g., learning arithmetic facts; reading an agreed-upon number of books; finding alternatives to fighting; making the bed or picking up toys when you are done playing).

It is important that goals be attainable within a relatively short time frame or younger children will tend to give up. Small goals that can be rather easily attained are preferable to those that take longer.

It is also important that goals be as specific as possible. For example, if a child says that his goal is to "be smart," you need to help him be much more specific. Goals should be both measurable and observable to the child. "Be smart" is too broad. "Learn my addition facts" or "learn the alphabet" are both measurable and observable. Most kids need frequent (even daily) assistance with goal development. As they get older and have more opportunity to practice, they may require less assistance. This practice will contribute to their overall ability to plan and organize tasks.

Activity for Kids...

Goals are things that we want to achieve. When we buy a model airplane or a puzzle, our goal is to put it together. But when we first open the box there are many pieces that don't look familiar. The parts or pieces we see look nothing like the finished picture on the box.

It is only after we read the directions (or have them read to us) or look at the pictures on the box that we can understand what we have to do to reach the *goal* (the completed model or puzzle). The directions are the *plan*. It is important that you get good at figuring out your *goals* and the *plans* you need to reach those goals. Kids who know their goals can feel good after their goals are achieved. Have you ever had a goal to clean up your room? How does it feel after you have cleaned it? Have you ever had a goal to finish reading a book? Doesn't it feel good when you've met that goal?

Setting goals helps you know when you have achieved something of value! Here's how:

1. Decide on a goal you want to reach.
MY GOAL IS _____
2. Decide on a plan you need to get you there. What are the steps you need to take? ("First I'll do this, then I'll do that.")
3. Check your plan with a parent, teacher or trusted friend .
4. Do each step in your plan, one at a time.
5. Reward yourself when you have reached your goal. (See "Reward Yourself" activity.)

Reward Yourself ■■■■■■■■■■■■■■■■■■■■■■■■■■■■■■

For Parents and Teachers...

Basic principles of behavior modification encourage parents and teachers to use positive reinforcement or rewards to strengthen desirable behavior. Most research has shown that it is better to reward good behavior than to punish bad behavior. Rewards typically fall into three categories: things, privileges and praise. They are given after a desired behavior has occurred. For example, "After your room is clean you can have your snack (thing) or watch TV (privilege)." A reward can simply be "I'm really proud of the good job you did in cleaning your room (praise)."

Kids feel good when special others notice and reward their efforts. But we need to be careful that they don't get too dependent on rewards. Ultimately, we want to teach them how to evaluate their own behavior so that they don't always need us around to tell them how they did. This next activity shows kids how they can reward themselves.

Parents and Teachers Can...

Assist children in compiling a list of desirable rewards. It is important to remember that self-esteem is more than the positive feeling from being recognized and complimented. It is primarily a belief in one's own capabilities.

You can help to promote positive self-esteem by saying things like, "I know how hard it must have been to control your temper when your sister (or another kid in class) made you mad. But you really did a fine job being in charge of yourself. What's on your reward list that you can give yourself for remembering to keep your cool?"

As a teacher or parent, you always want to find opportunities to acknowledge a child's development of mastery and control. Even when it seems that everything is bad, if you look hard enough, you'll find something that a child said or did that is deserving of some special, positive attention.

Activity for Kids...

1. Think about all of the things that you enjoy or feel good about. Lots of kids think about things like:

- Watching a favorite TV show or video.
- Taking a bike ride or a walk.
- Playing with a special friend.
- Playing sports.
- Going to a movie.
- Listening to music.
- Building a project.
- Getting a new toy or new clothes.
- Telling yourself "great job."

2. Write down the things you can think of on a piece of paper.

3. These are your rewards. Treat yourself to at least one reward every day after you have finished work or acted responsibly (completed chores, managed your temper even though Joe made you mad, completed your homework assignment, etc.). Decide your goal ("I'm going to get all of my arithmetic done.") and pick a reward ("I'll watch my favorite TV show after I've finished.").

4. Sometimes the best reward is to just remind yourself of something you did each day that made you feel proud. Tell yourself, "Today I felt proud of myself when I_____."

Being Your Own Best Friend ▪▪▪▫▫▫▫▫▫▫▫

For Parents and Teachers...

This activity teaches kids to be forgiving of themselves by reassuring themselves that they are okay. Hearing words of reassurance and feeling accepted by parents and teachers during troubled moments helps kids to keep their "imperfections" in the proper perspective.

Parents and Teachers Can...

As a parent or teacher, you can be the reassuring friend that children need during these troubled moments. As a friend you might use some of the suggestions offered by the following activity.

Activity for Kids...*

What do you say or do for your friends when they make mistakes or get mad at themselves? How do you react to them when things just aren't going well in their lives?

1. Most friends will say things like:

- ❦ "Don't worry, it's no big deal."
- ❦ "Forget about it."
- ❦ "You'll do better next time."
- ❦ "You can't always do your best."
- ❦ "Let's talk about it."
- ❦ "It can't be as bad as you think."
- ❦ "Let's go get a pizza."

2. Some friends might even give a little gift to a pal who is feeling kind of low. What are some other things that you might do for a friend when things aren't going well for him?
    a.
    b.
    c.
    d.

3. How about saying or doing some of these things to or for yourself when things aren't going right for you? You are the most important person there is, and you deserve to be at least as good to yourself as you might be to others. Just as you would say or do things to cheer up a friend, do the same for yourself.

---

* Adapted with permission from *Discipline with Dignity,* by R. Curwin and A. Mendler. Alexandria, VA: Association for Supervision and Curriculum Development, 1988. Also, in *Effective Discipline: Solving Problems at the Source.* Springhouse, PA: Learning Institute, 1988.

Using Positive Self-Talk■■■■■■■■■■■■■■■■||||||||

For Parents and Teachers...

When Louis plays three wrong notes at his violin recital, his father criticizes him for making the mistakes. Louis then tells himself that he is a lousy violin player and quits. Samantha turned in an excellent book report but forgot to put a period at the end of two sentences. Her teacher corrects the errors, and Samantha sits sulking in her chair for the whole day because her work isn't perfect. She has told herself that the only time she is smart enough is when she gets a perfect paper. James strikes out and his team loses. He calls himself a jerk! Bob's parents are getting divorced. He tells himself that if he was a better kid there would have been no problems and his parents would stay together.

All of these kids are having unhappy feelings, and they are silently saying negative things to themselves. The negative things they say make them feel even worse.

There are many minor problems encountered by children that they view as catastrophic. A bad grade, fear of parent criticism, peer rejection or a depressing segment on the nightly news can lead to sleepless nights filled with negative, ruminating thoughts. While there are indeed many events which understandably and appropriately lead to negative thoughts and feelings, most children are able to rebound quite quickly.

For others, however, the bad thoughts are like a snowball that quickly becomes an avalanche of catastrophe. These kids overreact to a bad situation by taking a true fact and drawing a false conclusion. A failing grade on a test is translated as "I must be stupid," instead of

"I feel bad about failing, but it's not the end of the world." Striking out three times in a ballgame becomes "I must stink...I'll never be called to play ball again," instead of "I really feel bad about letting the team down, but everyone has trouble sometimes."

Parents and Teachers Can...

Help kids who ruminate in the negative learn how to make a more realistic assessment of the facts. You can help by:

* Identifying recurrent themes which trouble the child (problems with friends, performance at school, relationships with family, etc.).
* Presenting an alternative way of thinking about problems by recognizing that something unpleasant has happened, not something catastrophic.
* Having the child practice aloud a new way of thinking about a problem ("I struck out three times. Too bad. I guess baseball's not my sport, maybe it's soccer." Or, "I struck out three times, so I should take some practice swings after school today to improve my hitting.")
* Being patient. It takes time and practice for somebody to learn how to view the world as a less catastrophic place.

Activity for Kids...

We can make ourselves feel better by learning how to say positive things to ourselves even when things don't go the way we want them to. Let's look at a list of positive words we can use to make us feel okay even when bad things happen:

* "It would be great if my parents stayed married. But I'm a kid and

kids can't control what parents do. It is a tough situation, but people who make it in life are those who can handle tough situations."

🐭 "I love getting good grades. But if I fail that spelling test tomorrow it won't be the end of the world. There'll be many more tests to take in my life and nobody can be perfect all of the time."

🐭 "I wish I could be as beautiful as Sarah. But hiding my face won't make it any prettier."

🐭 "I'm disappointed that I messed up the pass and the team lost. But teams win or lose as a group. I did the best I could, even though it didn't work out this time."

🐭 "It's too bad that I didn't play the violin as well as I could and that Dad is disappointed. I can't always make everybody happy."

Life would be great if good things always happened to us. But nobody's life is always smooth. When it gets bumpy, it is important that we:

Tell ourselves that it would be nice if things go the way we want; and

It isn't the end of the world when they don't!

There are very few things in life that are worth feeling miserable about.

Questions:

1. What are some things that are happening to you now that make you feel unhappy, worried, sad or angry?

2. What do you silently tell yourself that makes a bad situation even worse?

3. What can you tell yourself to improve the way you feel? "It would be nice if_____, but_____."

Nourishing Yourself and Others ▪▪▪▪▪▪▪

For Parents and Teachers...

It is exciting and fulfilling when people learn to notice each other's positive contributions. When kids hear other kids or grown-ups share how they made them feel good, self-esteem gets a big boost. This activity encourages people in groups (i.e., the family or classroom) to think about how other people around them have made them feel good.

Parents and Teachers Can...

Freely and frequently tell the child when she has done something or behaved in a manner that makes you feel good, proud and nourished. Have family meetings at home during which each family member states an appreciation about the contributions of others.

In the classroom, have the children sit in a circle. Ask each child to think of one or two classmates who made him feel good, as well as what specifically the classmate did. Give each child a turn to share, and encourage children to talk and share directly with each other.

When in a larger group, you'll want to be aware of children who get little positive feedback. Make a special point of telling them how they nourished you.

Activity for Kids...

Doesn't it feel great when other kids tell you that they think you're a good friend? How do you feel when you know you've done something good for someone else? How does it feel when someone else notices your good deed?

People have the power to help each other feel worthwhile and special. Little things can mean a lot: saying thanks to a friend who sticks up for you, complimenting someone's clothes, respecting another kid enough to invite him to play with you are some examples.

What are some other things that people sometimes say or do that make you feel good?

1.

2.

3.

4.

How about making sure that every day you do something to help somebody else feel good about himself? I'll bet you'll feel great in return.

Helping ▪▪▪▪▪▪▪▪▪▪▪▪▪▪▪▪▪▪▪▪▪▪▪▪▪▪▪▪▪▪▪▪▪▪▪▪▪

For Parents and Teachers...

"People who exercise vigorously often describe feeling high during a workout—and a sense of calmness and freedom from stress afterward.

New evidence reveals that these same emotional and physical changes can be produced with activity requiring much less exertion—helping others." So claims Allen Luks in an article in *Psychology Today* (Allan Luks, "Helper's High" [October 1988] 39-42). His reporting of research that analyzed the experiences of thousands of people further found that this "helper's calm" was linked to relief from stress-related disorders such as headaches, voice loss and even diseases such as lupus and multiple sclerosis.

There is no doubt that very positive and fulfilling feelings result when we help others who are less fortunate. It is, for example, remarkable to see toughened, delinquent youth dress up as clowns and entertain disabled children (as reported by Mr. Moe Bickweat, Facility Director, Oatka Residential Center, Industry, NY). Or to watch turned-off, angry students become helpers to younger children.

There is something wonderful and transforming that seems to grip the soul when people give of themselves to each other.

Parents and Teachers Can...

Encourage children to help others. Children can serve lunch in a soup kitchen for the homeless, play music for older citizens in a nursing home, help younger children read, tutor younger children, develop fund-raising efforts for a charitable cause.

If you are a teacher, one of the best strategies you can use with a turned-off student is to figure out a way for that child to contribute something of value to someone else.

Activity for Kids...

Volunteer your time to help others. At least once a week, make sure that you do something to benefit another person. Here are some ideas: visit a shut-in neighbor, maybe bring your pet too; offer to help an older neighbor shop; collect food for needy people; volunteer to be a "big" brother (sister) to a disabled child.

Not only will you be giving the most special of all gifts to another person (your time and attention), but you'll feel great inside too!

What ideas do you have to be a helper? As soon as you decide, make a plan and get started! Ask your parents for advice.

My helper ideas:

1.

2.

3.

4.

5.

Being Your Own Cop ∎∎∎∎∎∎∎∎∎∎∎∎∎∎∎∎∎∎∎∎

For Parents and Teachers...

This activity is designed to help children take responsibility for themselves and their own behavior. Kids get to see that they often have a lot more control over what happens to them than they think.

Even when others tell them what to do, it is important that they understand that they are still largely masters over how they feel and define themselves. It is very important that as parents and teachers we encourage our children to become good decision makers and help them see how the choices they make affect what happens to them.

I am reminded of a young boy, Kim, who seemed to be forever getting into trouble. Each time he was confronted, Kim would blame either circumstances or other people. Usually there was at least some measure of truth to his accusations, but it quickly became evident that Kim's blaming was primarily a familiar way for him to avoid responsibility for his actions. After all, it was always others who made him do it. Our focus became my gentle but firm insistence that Kim look at what he did and how he was contributing to problems on an event-by-event basis.

Then one day there was a breakthrough. As usual, Kim reported that he was in trouble at school. However, when I asked why, instead of avoiding responsibility he said, "'Cause I was shootin' paper clips, fightin' and I swore at the teacher." I congratulated Kim, whereupon he looked at me as if I were an alien who had just arrived from Mars.

He repeated, "I don't think you heard! I'm in trouble again!" And I said, "Right—but congratulations. Today it was *you* who made a decision to get into trouble, and while I'd prefer that you not, you made a *choice* and became a *decision maker.* You're even accepting the consequences. Making decisions is hard. Making good decisions is even harder!"

Parents and Teachers Can...

Help children identify "have tos." These are generally chores or responsibilities that are viewed as necessary to do so as to avoid disapproval or punishment from another. Too many "have tos" make kids feel pressured, while too few make them feel confused or anxious.

All kids need a structure that is defined by a knowing adult, along with freedom to pick and choose activities and interests. You can help your child by learning to balance "have tos" and "want tos." You can reinforce the idea of a favored interest or activity as a reward that follows the agony of a "have to" responsibility.

Activity for Kids...

Your mother says: "Pick up your mess right now."
Your dad says: "Late again! You're grounded for a week."
Your teacher says: "No homework again—another zero for you."
The police officer says: "You're busted—drugs in your locker."

Stop waiting for other people to lay down the law. You can like yourself a whole lot better when you become your own cop. Here's how:

1. Make a list of the things you "have to" do. Some of the things on your list might be "I have to make my bed every morning;" "I have to

walk the dog;" "I have to be in bed by 9:00 on weekdays;" "I have to make my bed every day." Write down as many things as you can think of that you have to do, either in the space below or on a separate piece of paper.

2. What happens to you when you don't do each of the things on your list? What are the consequences? Who plays cop?

3. Now instead of saying "I have to" to each of the things on your list, say "I want to" or "I choose to."

4. Saying "I want" or "I choose" gives you the power to be your own cop. Because if you decide not to do the homework or come home on time, then you have decided to allow the negative consequences to happen to you. You are in charge!

5. Reward yourself for taking responsibility for being your own cop. For example, when you choose to do your homework even though you'd prefer to be out playing with your friends, reward yourself for this choice.

Winning Reminders ■■■■■■■■■■▪▪▪▪▪▪▪▪▪▪▪▪▪▪▪▪▪

For Parents, Teachers and Kids...

It will help to remember that:

1. All people, even those who are the best at what they do, make mistakes. Kids who are winners are able to *hear* the criticism, *learn* from their errors and still feel good about themselves.

2. Winners know they can't make everybody happy all of the time.

3. Winners are able to change things that they can and accept things that they can't change. When work gets tough, they double their effort. When other people don't always approve of them, they understand that no one is wonderful in everyone's eyes.

4. Winners who have parents or teachers with problems are able to turn off bad things said to them. They don't accept words like lazy, stupid, careless just because a powerful grown-up has said that to them. They understand that grown-ups who say such things really have bigger problems that have nothing to do with the kid.

5. Winners do lots to reward themselves; they help other people; they choose to be responsible; and they allow time for fun.

Chapter 2

Ways to Make Your Mind and Body Relax

To Parents and Teachers

Children, like adults, differ in temperament, with some being more naturally calm and relaxed as they allow the proverbial water to roll off their backs, while others are high strung. These differences are even observable in a newborn nursery, with some infants kicking and screaming from the moment of birth. Others appear quiet and placid.

While research to discover the main determinants of stress is inconclusive, it is safe to say that a combination of innate temperamental factors and what we learn from others defines each individual's ability to tolerate stress. We do know that even those who are high strung can learn to make themselves feel calmer.

Until fairly recently it was believed that the autonomic nervous system (ANS), which becomes quite active when we are stressed, was beyond our control. Sweaty hands, increased heart rate, a rise in blood pressure, secretion of hormones from the adrenal glands that arouse our bodies and dilation of the pupils are just some of the physiological reactions caused when the ANS is stimulated.

While appropriate arousal of the ANS is desirable and in fact necessary for survival, a frequently overaroused system can lead to various cardiovascular or gastrointestinal problems, especially in adults. The seeds for many stress-related problems are sown in childhood.

Recent research has conclusively demonstrated that many previously thought involuntary reactions can in fact be monitored and controlled. We can learn to slow down our heart rate, regulate the amount of blood that flows to different parts of our bodies, increase or decrease blood pressure and make lots of our body muscles relax. In short, we have much more control over how our body functions than had been previously believed.

The first activity in this chapter helps children learn how to identify their feelings and introduces them to a concept called an "I-statement," which demonstrates how to directly express these feelings to others. The remaining activities in the chapter are designed to help children learn how to quiet their minds and bodies, thereby producing a feeling of relaxation.

Children who worry a lot, who can't settle down, who are distractible or hyperactive, who have difficulty focusing their attention, or who have difficulty falling asleep may find these activities especially beneficial. Some kids who use medications for calming may find in these activities an equally effective, alternative way to relax.

Most children can increase their stress tolerance by practicing these activities. All activities require practice and should be done several times (once or twice every day for 10-15 minutes each) for maximum benefit.

As a parent or teacher you can assist by:

❧ Suggesting activities based upon your knowledge of a child.
❧ Reading the activity in a quiet, soothing tone of voice while the child practices.
❧ Providing a tape recording of your child's favorites, either by asking a friend with a soothing voice, doing it yourself or having the child make his own. In this way your child can practice whenever he wants.

Parents and Teachers Can...

Assist children in deciding the effectiveness of the strategies in this chapter by thoroughly explaining how to use the Relaxing Rating Scale in the appendix. Helping kids think in opposites (hot-cold, happy-sad, tense-calm) enables them to understand how to label their feelings. Since most people, including kids, don't feel all these feelings at any given time, the continuum is a suggested way in which small changes in feelings can be measured.

You can also use the scale to rate children's tension-relaxation on the basis of your own observations. Finally, you can enjoy and derive the same benefits from these activities by doing them either alone or along with a child. The first activity in this section is designed to help children identify and express their feelings.

To Kids

Making ourselves feel relaxed is usually a lot easier than we think. Would you believe that something as simple as breathing in nice deep breaths can make most of us feel calm and relaxed? Before you decide whether or not that works for you, it is first important to learn how to label the feelings you have. Sometimes it is even a good idea to tell other people exactly how you feel.

The first activity in this chapter teaches how to do these things. After that, I'd like to suggest that you use the Relaxing Rating Scale (use a pencil so you can reuse it) in Appendix A. The rating scale can be used for all the rest of the activities in this chapter. The idea of the scale is the same as the ratings you did with "smiling" and "fun" in chapter 1. You can decide which of the activities work best for you. Keep in mind that you'll need to practice these exercises several times before they begin to work really well for you. But you'll probably notice yourself becoming more calm and relaxed soon after you begin.

Ways to Make Your Mind and Body Relax

Feelings ▪▪▪▪▪▪▪▪▪▪▪▪▪▪▪▪▪▪▪▪▪▪▪▪▪▪▪▪▪▪

For Parents and Teachers...

It is important that kids understand *how* to identify their feelings, *why* that is important and then how to *express* feelings. There is a direct relationship between how we feel and how we behave. When we feel angry we are more likely to fight. When we feel afraid, we are more likely to be quiet by withdrawing. Adults probably smoke and drink more when tense.

The basic feelings that all people have are: happiness (also known as joy), sadness (also known as disappointment), fear (also known as worry, nervousness, anxiety), excitement (also known as energy, enthusiasm, liveliness) and anger (also known as being mad, frustration).

When kids can identify and more fully express their feelings verbally, it is less likely that they will build up stress. Furthermore, they learn an effective way to tell themselves and others about their inner experience. Doing that helps kids to feel more positively connected with others. This contributes directly to self-esteem.

Parents and Teachers Can...

Be good "feeling" models. It is difficult for many of us to identify and effectively express our feelings. It is not unusual to push down or suppress feelings, especially when they aren't pleasant. However, kids really appreciate and deepen their respect for us when we show our human side.

We can do this by directly and honestly telling our kids how we feel. Use I-statements. These include three components (More detailed information about this is found in *Parent Effectiveness Training* by Thomas Gordon. New York: Peter H. Wyden, 1972.):

1. Say how you feel.
2. Say what happened to make you feel that way.
3. Say what you will or might do about it.

To show how that works, let's say you get home from work and you're feeling tense and frustrated. Your son sees you and says, "Hi Mom, how are you?" An example of an I-statement is "Son, I feel very tense right now. There were some difficult things that happened at work. Right now, I am going to take a warm, relaxing bath. As soon as I'm through, I want to hear all about your day."

In a classroom setting, you can generate a list of feeling words along with pictures of kids showing these feelings. That helps both to teach and remind children of feelings. Teach I-statements by giving kids sample situations and have them practice reacting to them.

Activity for Kids...

How do you feel when your parents forget to do something they promised? You probably feel angry. When you are faced with a tough school assignment and you don't know where to begin, you probably feel frustrated. When the teacher calls on you and you don't have the answer, you feel embarrassed.

It is usually okay to tell people how you feel because when you do it gives them a chance to change their behavior. Even if they don't, at least you can be sure that they know that something they did is bugging you.

If you don't tell how you feel then people won't know, and they may keep right on doing things that you don't like. Then you'll probably get mad and maybe even start a fight, call someone a name and eventually get into trouble.

Before the troubles start, try *telling* people how you feel. Use an I-statement. It takes practice to really get good at I-statements because you have to:

1. Say how you feel. ("I feel_____")

2. Say why you feel the way you do. ("because _____")

3. Tell what you're going to do about it. ("and I want/I will_____")

For example, Manuel calls Joey a "nerd." Joey decides to use an I-statement. He says, "Manuel, I get mad when you call me names because that hurts my feelings and I want you to stop." If manuel does not stop, Joey can say, "If you don't stop I'll tell the teacher."

Sample Problems:

Practice using I-statements.

1. Sean is left out by a group of kids on the playground. How does he feel? Pretend you are Sean; make an I-statement to one or some of the friends.

2. Cassandra works hard and gets excellent grades. Nicole and Laura laugh at her and say unkind things. Have Cassandra make an I-statement to the girls.

3. David's dad has been drinking a lot, and when he's drunk he does and says scary things. On a recent day in class, David's teacher,

Mrs. Gonzalez, said to him in private, "David, you seem unhappy. What's bothering you?" Pretend you are David; use an I-statement to answer Mrs. Gonzalez's question.

Music Listening ▪▪▪▪▪▪▪▪▪▪▪▪▪▪▪▪▪▪▪▪▪▪▪▪▪▪▪▪

For Parents and Teachers...

Many children and adults find music soothing. The calming effects of music have been demonstrated and have led to many audiotapes that are readily available. Some contain only music while others have relaxation-associated sounds such as the ocean, chirping birds or other sounds of nature.

Parents and Teachers Can...

Encourage children to relax with music. Even in the classroom, children can be permitted to listen through headphones as they either relax or do their work. Visit bookstores and/or record shops with your child and ask to listen to the "relaxing" musical tapes.

Activity for Kids...

Lots of times people relax by listening to music. Even babies do. If you have a baby brother or sister you may have heard your mom sing softly to the baby as a way of getting the baby to become quiet or to fall asleep. Maybe your mom still sings to you each night at bedtime.

Some music makes us feel alive and stimulated. Some music creates drama. And some music is especially there to help us relax.

Now, it is up to you to decide if music is relaxing for you and what type of music you find relaxing. If you aren't sure, then the next time you are in a record store, ask the salesperson about tapes that have relaxing sounds. Maybe you can listen right there in the store.

You also could listen to different radio stations so that you get to know about different types of music. You may discover new kinds of music to enjoy. Ask your parents or teacher to help.

Ways to Make Your Mind and Body Relax ———————————— 41

Breathing for Relaxation▪■■■■■▬▬▬▬▬▬||||||||||||||||

For Parents and Teachers...

Some years ago, a famous doctor (Dr. Herbert Benson), wrote a book for grown-ups called *The Relaxation Response* (Avon Books, 1976). He found that when adults did an exercise that was suggested in his book, they felt more relaxed and good things actually happened to their bodies. Many young people also enjoy this activity. Dr. Benson tells adults that they'll feel best when they do this two times a day for five or ten minutes each time.

I have included Dr. Benson's technique, which is the third of three breathing activities. There are many variations of breathing exercises that are associated with relaxation, and I have simply included my favorites.

It is important to note that when most adults and children first begin these kinds of exercises, it is very common for them to have trouble sustaining their concentration. As you will see in the directions, when expected distractions occur, the child is instructed to leave the distracting thought and return his attention to the breathing.

Parents and Teachers Can...

Do these exercises! Your success with them will communicate their credibility to kids. Tell your family that you will be taking time for relaxing (a few minutes) and that you need to be in a quiet place with nobody disturbing you during that time. You can invite your children to join you so that you can practice relaxing together. Be sure to explain and model how to do it, as well as to point out problems with distraction that many people have in the beginning.

Breathing Activity #1 for Kids...*

1. Sit in a comfortable chair.

2. Pay attention to how you breathe. Relaxed breathing is slow and deep.

3. Close your eyes and slowly breathe in through your nose, sending all the air deep into your lungs and stomach.

4. Slowly breathe out through your nose and mouth, and as you do, allow all of the tension (tightness, butterflies in your stomach, etc.) to leave your body through the breath that comes out.

5. Keep doing this for five minutes.

6. At the end of the five minutes, slowly open your eyes and remain seated for another moment or two.

7. Slowly get out of your chair and go about doing whatever your plans call for.

8. Enjoy the calmer, quieter, more relaxing way you feel.

* Reprinted with permission from *Discipline with Dignity* by Robert Curwin and Allen Mendler. Alexandria, VA: Association for Supervision and Curriculum Development, 1988. Also, in *Effective Discipline: Solving Problems at the Source.* Springhouse, PA: Learning Institute, 1988.

Breathing Activity #2 for Kids...

1. Close your eyes as you sit in a comfortable spot, and as you breathe in through your nose, silently count from one to five.

2. When you reach five, hold your breath to the count of five.

3. Now slowly breathe out as you silently count to five.

4. After you reach five and all the air has been breathed out, count silently from one to five before you breathe in again.

5. Keep doing this for at least five minutes.

Breathe in one...two...three...four...five.

Hold your breath one...two...three...four...five.

Breathe out one...two...three...four...five.

Hold one...two...three...four...five.

Breathe in again one...two...three...four...five.

6. At the end of the five minutes, slowly open your eyes and enjoy the calm, relaxed feeling.

7. Slowly get out of your chair and go about doing whatever your plans call for.

Breathing Activity #3 for Kids...

You can try the breathing exercise suggested by Dr. Herbert Benson, too.

1. Sit in a comfortable chair in a quiet place where you won't be disturbed for five or ten minutes.

2. Close your eyes and breathe in through your nose.

3. As you breathe out, say silently to yourself the number "one."

4. Breathe in again, and as before, each time you breathe out say the number "one."

5. After five or ten minutes, end the activity by opening your eyes slowly, sitting in your chair calmly for another minute with your eyes open, and then slowly leaving your chair as your return to doing anything you want.

Some prefer other relaxing words such as "quiet, peaceful, calm, happy." Try different ones. Use what works well for you.

Note to Kids:

Most kids (and grown-ups too) who do this and most of the other "quiet" activities in this book say that when they first start doing them, they have some trouble just saying the number "one" or paying attention to their breathing as required in Exercise #1.

If that happens to you all you have to do is: as soon as you catch your thoughts drifting (the baseball game, homework that needs to get finished, chores around the house, etc.), just leave that thought and return your attention to quietly saying your relaxing word. After a few days of practice, this should be less and less of a problem.

Stare to Sleep ■■■■■■■■■■■■■■■■■■■■■■■■■■■■■■■■■■■■■

For Parents and Teachers...

This next activity provides a way for children to relax and often fall asleep when they otherwise can't. One of the leading concerns that many parents have as a child grows has to do with sleep. At one time or another, most children will have difficulty falling asleep. For some, specific concerns about family, friends or school will keep them tossing and turning.

Younger children sometimes stay awake worrying about monsters and the bogeyman. Certainly, providing reassurance, support and being a good listener at those times can itself help a child become calmer.

Many other children who have trouble sleeping do not feel nervous or anxious nor are they able to identify any reason for this difficulty. Some children go through cycles in which they will struggle with sleep for weeks or even months at a time. While not a "cure-all" for all children, I have found that "Stare to Sleep" can assist many in slowing their mental energy so that sleep may follow.

Parents and Teachers Can...

Approach most sleep problems in a matter-of-fact, calm, reassuring manner. It helps to let kids know that trouble falling asleep is normal and that just about everybody goes through it. Most children are sufficiently resourceful that they will invent ways to assist themselves to sleep with your help. Listening to a radio or relaxing tape and reading until tired are other strategies that kids may find helpful.

Teachers can use this activity as a way to show children how to relax in school and/or as a way to assist with sleep at home. In fact, my 9-year-old son taught this activity to me after a teacher had taught him a variation in his class.

A professional consultation is advised when sleep problems persist, especially when there are also eating problems (poor appetite or overeating), low energy or fatigue, poor concentration or generally low self-esteem.

Activity for Kids...

1. Lie down in your bed on your back when it's time for sleep. This activity is very good to do if you have some trouble falling asleep at night.

2. As you rest on your bed, look at a spot on the ceiling. The spot can be a speck of dirt, a chip in the paint or anything else you see. Be sure to either find a small spot or to notice just a very small part of the ceiling.

3. After you have your spot, keep looking at it. Look only at your spot, and you'll soon notice that your eyes begin to feel watery and tired. Allow your eyes to close when they become so tired of looking that they just can't stay open any more.

4. With your eyes closed, silently tell yourself, "I am falling asleep. I am falling into a deep, calm sleep." Repeat this to yourself a few times.

Relaxing Your Whole Body ▬▬▬▭▭▭▭▭▭

For Parents and Teachers...

When things bother us, different parts of the body may feel tight or tense. Your shoulders or neck may feel stiff, your stomach may be jittery, your hands may feel restless, or you may have a headache. You can learn to relax each part of your body to feel great.

Parents Can...

Help kids quiet and calm themselves by providing structured *quiet time* in the home. My family began this after observing our 11 year old gulping down his dinner every night so that he could rush out and play with his friends who were shooting baskets in my driveway during dinnertime. On nasty days the phone rang endlessly, disrupting all conversation, not to mention my digestion. I finally realized that an older son, talented in music, was resenting having to practice while his brother and friends were out there socializing.

We developed a *quiet time* between 5:15 and 6:45 each evening. There is no TV permitted, no friends allowed over and no phone calls accepted during this time. It is a time for dinner, family discussion, homework, quiet reading, practicing music or doing relaxation activities.

Not only don't my kids complain (the 11 year old lodged a mild initial protest), they actually look forward to this structured time. And my digestion has improved at least a hundred fold!

Teachers Can...

This and many of the other activities in this chapter can be used as a way of moving from high physical energy (for example, after gym or recess) to a more quiet, focused activity (such as math). It is also encouraging to note that some researchers have found that these activities can make a positive difference in the attention span and concentration shown by children identified with "attention deficit hyperactivity disorder."

Activity for Kids...

1. Sit up straight in a comfortable chair with your hands in your lap and your feet on the floor. Close your eyes.

2. *Tense* or *tighten* or *squeeze* the muscles in your feet, legs and toes as tightly as you can. Silently count to five as you hold this position. Then release and stretch out those muscles.

3. Now go to the muscles of your chest and stomach. Tighten up those muscles as you silently count to five, then relax.

4. Go to your arms, fingers and shoulders. Tighten up these muscles. Silently count to five, then let go. Feel the relaxation.

5. Now go to your head and neck. Scrunch up the muscles of your face as you count to five, then relax those muscles. Do it again and make sure that you scrunch your mouth, nose, eyes and teeth, and then relax each of those parts of your body.

6. Now go back to your feet and do all of your body again. Squeeze or tighten each body part, count to five, then relax. When you finish, open your eyes and notice how relaxed your whole body feels.

Guided Pictures ■■■■■■■■■■■■■■■■■■■■■■■■■■■■■■■■■■

For Parents and Teachers...

The next few activities suggest different pictures or stories that make many kids feel calm and relaxed. Most of us have read some books or seen TV shows that have become our favorites. Usually there is a lot of action, as in exciting, fast-moving pictures like *Batman, Star Wars* or *Indiana Jones*. When we leave these kinds of movies, we often feel excited all over and our hearts may be thumping quickly.

Just as some movies cause excitement, others can be calming. Like the breathing activities, learning how to make relaxing mental pictures can quiet a racing mind. If children have trouble sitting still at school or concentrating on their work, practicing these pictures may be helpful. They can also help children to relax enough to fall asleep. Some older kids who used to do drugs tell me that these kinds of mental pictures make them feel as good as they did when they took drugs.

Even if kids don't have any of these problems, they'll probably enjoy creating these pictures in their own minds. There are three different guided fantasy activities presented.

Parents and Teachers Can...

Help provide structure and guidance around these types of activities. It is usually best to have somebody else read each of these suggested pictures to kids in a relaxed, enjoyable, story-telling way.

You or someone with a soothing voice can even make a tape recording of the activity. Kids who are old enough to read can do this too, then listen to their own voice. Have children keep their eyes closed and provide a place that is free of any distractions.

Before you actually do the activity, it often helps for participants to get into a relaxed state of mind by doing one of the breathing activities in this chapter. I would also suggest that you do any or all of these guided pictures so that you too can achieve the benefits associated with these activities.

Blackboard Picture for Kids...*

(Note: younger children may be unable to pay attention for this long. Use fewer numbers with shorter pauses with younger children.)

Picture a blackboard in front of you with a piece of chalk resting on the ledge underneath the board. Keeping your eyes closed while you sit in a comfortable chair or lie in your soft bed, picture yourself walking slowly toward the blackboard.

When you get to the blackboard, pick up the chalk and in the upper left hand corner of the blackboard, write the number 10 (pause). Next to the number 10 write the word *relax* (pause ten seconds).

Underneath the number 10, write down the number 9, and next to the 9 write the word *calm* (pause ten seconds).

Under the nine write the number 8, and next to the 8 write the word *peaceful* (pause ten seconds).

Write the number 7 under the 8, and next to the 7 write the word *quiet* (pause ten seconds).

Write the number 6, and next to the 6 write the word *soft* (pause ten seconds).

Write the number 5 under the 6, and next to the 5 write the words *very relaxed* (pause fifteen seconds).

Write the number 4 under the 5, and next to the 4 write the words *very calm* (pause fifteen seconds).

Write the number 3 under the 4, and next to the 3 write the words *very soft* (pause fifteen seconds).

Write the number 2 under the 3, and next to the 2 write down *very quiet* (pause fifteen seconds).

Write the number 1 under the 2, and next to the 1 write the words *very very relaxed* (pause twenty seconds).

You should now be feeling very calm, quiet and relaxed and as soon as you want to end the fantasy and return your attention to the room, just count from 1 to 5.

You will feel very relaxed but also awake and alert by the time you reach 5. When you reach 5, open your eyes and notice how you feel. If you want to use this to help you fall asleep, just let yourself drift off into a nice, deep sleep.

---

* *An adaptation of this activity was introduced to the author at a workshop with Edith Saiki sponsored by the Drug and Alcohol Council in Rochester, NY.*

Magic Carpet Picture for Kids...

Picture in front of you a soft, fluffy, thick piece of carpet (pause).... The carpet looks so comfortable that you can now actually picture yourself lying on it (pause).... Feel how soft, warm and fluffy it is (pause)....

As you rest on your fluffy piece of carpet, you notice that it is magical. It actually talks in a soft, calm voice and tells you it is about to take you on a wonderful ride (pause).... You can feel yourself slowly being lifted off the ground by the magic carpet underneath you.

It is so magical that it keeps you safe and supported even as it floats in the air (pause)....

Notice how this carpet takes you above the houses and over the land and up into the clouds on a warm, quiet day (pause).... You can hear birds singing as the warm breeze passes over you (pause).... Feel yourself calmly floating in the air aboard your magic carpet (pause)....

Now you begin to notice how it slowly gets lower and lower, passing under the clouds and heading toward a soft landing on the ground. You and your magic carpet touch the ground just as softly as a feather would land (pause)....

Your magic carpet has taken you to the most beautiful place you have ever been. You can smell the sweet smell of flowers, hear the chirping sounds of birds at play (pause).... You can feel the soft green grass under your feet as you walk about feeling as light as a feather (pause)....

You are in charge at this place. Maybe you see people or heroes there that you like (pause).... Look around—if they aren't there, you have the power to make them appear or disappear (pause)....

Stay there another moment and add anything to your magical place that you want (pause).... In a few moments you'll return to your magic carpet for your flight home (pause)....

It is now time to leave so say goodbye for now. You know that you can return another time if you want (pause).... Get onto your magic carpet and once again feel it lift off as it did before—slowly, calmly and safely (pause)....

Above the ground, up and through the clouds you float (pause).... Notice how you begin to get closer and closer to home as you float down through the clouds. You can see your house as you get closer and closer (pause)....

You are now home safely. Your ride has come to an end, but you have the power to take yourself back to that special place again (pause)....

Whenever you feel ready, open your eyes and return to being where you are. Continue to enjoy the peaceful feeling of relaxation and notice how calm, quiet, yet alert you are.

Troubles Balloon Picture for Kids...

Picture in front of you a very large hot-air balloon with a big passenger basket attached to the bottom (pause).... The hot-air balloon is in an open field, tied to the ground with thick rope.

Picture yourself walking toward this hot-air balloon, and as you come closer you see a sign that says, *"Dump all of your problems and troubles into the basket"* (pause)....

You are allowed to place anything you want into the basket. You are taking a vacation from your troubles and problems, so anything that gives you a problem can be put into the basket. Maybe you want to put your teacher in there or another kid who has been mean to you. Maybe you want to put your mom or dad or brother or sister or some other person in there. Maybe you want to throw your chores in there, or a disappointing report card.

This basket has enough room for as many troubles as you have. Perhaps you want to load up the basket with the tears, anger or frustration inside you (pause).... Dump it all in (pause)....

Now cut the rope that has held the balloon on the ground and watch as the balloon begins to lift off the ground. It gets higher and higher as your troubles move farther and farther away (pause).... Watch it until it becomes as small as a speck and then disappears completely from sight (pause)....

Your troubles have left for awhile. Enjoy the feeling of lightness that comes over you as you enjoy your troubles-free vacation.

Chapter 3

Letting Off Steam

To Parents and Teachers

One of the most difficult skills for children to learn is distinguishing between *feelings* and *actions*. It is one's inability to accept oneself as a feeling person that leads to either self-defeating behavior that is harmful to oneself or harmful actions directed against others.

Drinking alcohol, using drugs, excessive worrying and purposeful failure are but a few of the self-defeating ways that people turn their feelings against themselves. Frequent fighting, loss of temper and bullying against those less powerful are inappropriate ways in which unpleasant feelings are directed outward.

It is incumbent upon parents and teachers to encourage their children to become aware of and alive to their feelings by teaching the difference between "bad feelings" and "bad actions." As much as we'd like our kids to always entertain loving thoughts and feelings, a more realistic proposition is for them to learn that anger, resentment and hate can be felt without causing harm to either themselves or others.

As such, all thoughts and feelings are considered acceptable. It is only *behavior* or *actions* that are open to question. Children can learn that feeling angry or sad is okay but that hitting someone or drugging away sadness is not.

The activities in this chapter provide relief from unpleasant stress by teaching children several safe outlets by which they can express their feelings without hurting themselves or others.

Children are taught:

❧ That it is okay to feel unpleasant feelings and to sometimes think unkind thoughts.

- That it is better for them to release these feelings in a safe way than it is to either keep them locked inside or hurt others.
- That letting off steam will often make them feel less tense and they will then be better able to think up a good solution to a problem.
- That not all problems can be easily solved, but even when problems won't go away, there are things they can do to reduce the stress that these problems cause.

For maximum benefit, children need to know that you approve of their engaging in these activities. They may initially feel uneasy about doing such things as screaming into or pounding pillows, talking to an empty chair and twisting or biting a towel.

Adults often feel uncomfortable at first with these kinds of activities as well. However, most kids and adults report beneficial effects after they overcome their initial reluctance. Read through each of the activities. Try some or all of them. Assess the effects. Then help children become acquainted with all of the activities or guide the activity selections on the basis of what is comfortable for you and what you believe might be helpful to your kids.

To Kids

- Do you ever get so mad that you feel you might explode?
- Have you ever wanted to cry when the bully on the bus threatens to get the whole class to beat you up?
- Do you sometimes want to swear at a parent or hurt your little sister?
- Have you ever felt like tearing your homework or schoolbook into a thousand pieces?
- Have you ever thought about doing something to anger your friend who is now playing with your ex-friend?

There are times when all people are so filled with rage or fear that if they actually did what they wanted to do, it would make things worse. In fact, there are some boys and girls (grown-ups too) who hurt other people or destroy property when they can't control these feelings. Most feel bad afterward, but then it's too late.

When normal feelings of rage, anger or fear build up inside of you, you need to learn how to *safely let off steam.*

Letting off steam means doing things to get rid of these strong feelings before they get you into trouble. None of us can make good decisions when our feelings are so strong. So before we decide how to deal with the situation or person who makes us feel upset, we need to make these strong feelings weaker.

All of the activities in this chapter are to help when you are feeling *very* tense or stressed.

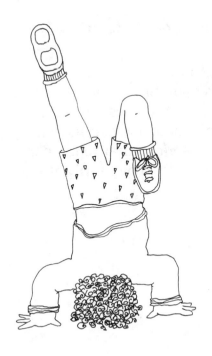

Accept All of Your
Thoughts and Feelings▬▬▬▬▬▬▬▬▬▬▬

For Parents and Teachers...

All kids experience angry feelings and have occasional desires to hurt others, especially when they feel unfairly treated or blocked from doing something they want.

Many kids keep these feelings bottled inside because they are afraid of losing love, respect and acceptance if they express these thoughts. The anger then turns to guilt, and children may find ways to punish themselves for their "bad" thoughts.

Parents and Teachers Can...

Help by letting children know that you understand their feelings. Explain that all kids sometimes *hate* people they mostly love, such as their parents, other loved ones or teachers. Having these feelings does not make them bad. Help children by providing an outlet to safely express these feelings that leads neither to violence nor guilt. Many kids are greatly helped by simply articulating their inner thoughts to a caring listener.

Activity for Kids...

Do not feel guilty about any of your thoughts or feelings. Right and wrong only has to do with how you act, not with how you feel or what you think. It is even normal and okay to sometimes *think* about hurting your parents, teachers or other kids. It is *not* okay to actually hurt the person or destroy someone's property.

There are times when things can seem very confusing. When we are very little we expect grown-ups to know and act better than we do. So if a grown-up does or says something unkind, most kids think that they must be to blame.

Let me tell a story about something that happened to me. When I was in third grade, everybody in class was given a test. When the tests were graded, my teacher had each kid in the class stand in a line according to how we did. In other words, the kid who did best was called first and became the first in line. Each kid was called until the kid who did worst stood last in line. I was called next to last! How do you think I felt? That's right! I felt terrible, angry and embarrassed. I also thought that I must be stupid. "After all," I thought, "my teacher is smart and if I did so bad on the test, I must be dumb!"

Now that I'm a grown-up, I am able to see that teachers and parents sometimes make mistakes. Even though they seem strong and perfect, they can say or do things that can be hurtful and wrong. Sometimes I say things to my own kids that I regret.

Some kids unfortunately have parents or teachers who never think they do anything right. Those kids really need a friend to remind them that they are just as terrific as anyone else. Be a friend and show others how to let off steam, by sharing these ideas and activities.

Asking Questions▪▪▪▪▪▪▪▪▪▪▪▪▪▪▪▪▪▪▪▪▪▪▪▪▪▪▪▪▪▪

For Parents and Teachers ...

Sometimes "steam," the boiling feeling inside that stress can cause, builds up when kids have questions that they are either afraid to ask or don't know how to ask. They may feel that if they ask the questions then their fears will come true. Even worse, they may fear the answer they will get.

For example, it is quite normal for kids of about 7 to 9 years to worry about the death or divorce of their parents. Children will have such worries even if the thought of divorce has never been mentioned by either parent. Although children sometimes fear asking the question, they almost always feel relieved after sharing their concerns with a good listener.

Parents and Teachers Can...

Make it easier for kids to formulate and ask questions. Be aware of a child's recent experiences (e.g., seeing a scary movie), current emotional climate in the family and stage of development. If you have a hunch that the child is burdened with a question she's not asking, explore your hunch verbally with the child. You might try:

1. (Child's name), you seem concerned about something. Is there anything you'd like to say or ask?

2. When I was your age, I remember wondering about _____. Do you ever wonder in that way?

3. Many kids your age have questions about _____.
Does that ever cross your mind?

Leave the door open! If you get no response, say with acceptance, "If you get to thinking about _____, I hope you'll feel comfortable asking me about it." Finally, there's an excellent book by Dr. Gregory Stock called *The Kid's Book of Questions (1)* that may help your child to explore a current concern.

Activity for Kids...

One of the best things that you can do for yourself is to ask questions when there are things that you don't understand. Questions are like feelings—you can't just push them away. You will keep wondering until you get an answer.

Not all questions have easy answers, but that should not stop you from asking. Let some trusted adult know what's on your mind. And if you aren't satisfied with an answer, then ask somebody else the question. Ask yourself the following questions. Some will have more than one answer.

Questions:

1. What questions do I have about school? Friends? My family?

2. What questions do I have about how people treat each other?

3. What are some other questions I have? _____

_____

Pillow Pounding ■■■■■■■■■■■■■■■■■■■■■■■IIIIIIIIIIIIIIIIIIIIIIIIIIIIII

For Parents and Teachers...

Help children understand the activity and its purpose. Then check in with the child after the activity by using the following guide:

❧ How do you feel right now (more or less calm)? This is important for you to ascertain because there are some children who may actually become more aggressive or tense when doing this and the next two activities.

❧ Acknowledge that punching a pillow may not feel quite as good as the real thing, but reinforce the idea that settling problems through violence only leads to more violence.

❧ Tell your child, "Now that you've unloaded a lot of angry feelings, let's think together about some ways to tell people how you feel instead of either punching them or a pillow" (see Chapters 1 and 4).

Activity for Kids...

Sometimes you feel so angry that your body gets really tight. Your fists want to hit or your legs want to kick. You may even want to go after someone who has hurt your feelings.

Try this instead:

1. Go to a room where you won't be bothered.

2. Get a big fluffy pillow (one from the couch or the one you sleep on would be okay).

3. Imagine or pretend that the pillow is really the person that you feel mad at.

4. Look at the pillow and picture the person's face and body.

5. Pound away with your fists against the pillow as you let your anger pour through your whole body into your fists while you continue to picture the person. If you can't picture someone, that's okay. You may still get to feeling calmer by getting out your tension in this way.

6. Keep doing this until you feel more calm.

7. After you have finished, try one of the activities from Chapter 2 (relaxing your body) to feel even more relaxed.

Pillow Screaming ■■■■■■■■■■■■■■■■■■■■■■■■■

For Parents and Teachers...

If a child is swearing, yelling or screaming at you and you find yourself about to scream back, try to remember that doing so is most likely to lead to more conflict and a power struggle.

You can say instead, "Jessica, you are so angry that you need to scream. I'd like to hear your complaints, and I will when you can speak to me more calmly. Why don't you go to another room and do as much screaming and swearing into a pillow as you want? When you're finished, we'll get together and talk." Incidentally, you (parent or teacher) might want to go to another room for a little screaming as well!

Activity for Kids...

When it is a real struggle for you *not* to scream, stop struggling. Let it out safely. The other day I was playing tennis with my son and he just wasn't playing well. We all have those days. After about the tenth shot that he hit into the net, he looked around and noticing that nobody except me was around, he let out a loud one-second scream that seemed to come from his toes, all the way through his stomach and out of his mouth.

Afterward, we just looked at each other, laughed, and got back to playing. If other people were nearby, it wouldn't have been appropriate or thoughtful for him to do that.

Most of the time, kids are around other people. So if you're frustrated and you want to scream it out, try doing the following:

In a room by yourself, take a pillow and press it lightly over your own face. With the pillow held up against your face, scream into it. Scream as loud as you want because the pillow will block most of the sound. You won't have to worry about upsetting anybody else.

But in case you are worried that somebody will be concerned or think you are wacky, tell them that you'll be "screaming out some anger or madness." You might say something like, "Mom, I'm really upset right now. I'll be in the other room screaming. There's nothing to worry about. As soon as I feel better, I'll be back."

Empty Chair ████████████████████████████████

For Parents and Teachers...

This exercise provides a less physical means for releasing feelings than pillow pounding. It helps kids to become quite clear about who they are upset with and why they feel as they do. Since the long-range goal is to teach assertiveness (see Chapter 4), this exercise provides a bridge between *pillow pounding, pillow screaming* and the problem-solving activities in the next chapter.

Just as one might practice telling off the boss before actually doing so, the "Empty Chair" activity gives kids a chance both to let go of excess tension and practice what they want to say before they actually do anything.

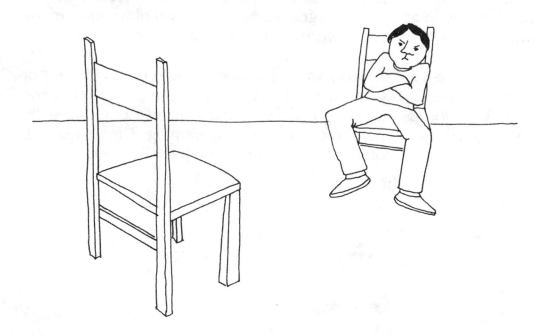

Activity for Kids...

1. Sit in a chair and place an empty chair across from you so that you are looking right at it.

2. Now picture the person who is making you feel angry, sad or upset seated in that empty chair.

3. Tell the person in the chair all of the things he does that bother you or that make you feel upset. (I hate it when_____. It bothers me when_____. What you do that upsets me is_____.)

4. Keep going until you feel finished.

5. Now that you have told this person in the chair your gripes, think about what you might really want to say to this person the next time you see him. Try to figure out how that person might react to what you say. It is difficult to learn how to talk so that other people will really listen. Some of the suggestions I gave in Chapter 2 on I-statements will help.

Later in this book you'll learn even more about sending I-statements that can help with some upsetting people.

Towel Twisting or Biting ▄▄▄▄▄▄▄▄▄▄▄▄▄▄▄▄▄▄▄

For Parents and Teachers...

A famous college basketball coach can be seen on TV with a towel when his team plays a game. During close games or when his players make mistakes, this coach will often have the towel twisted as he bites on it. My guess is that he sometimes feels like biting a player after a bad play or a referee after a call that goes against his team. But how long do you think he could keep his job if he went around biting players and referees during the games?

The towel provides a non-harmful outlet for his aggressive feelings. In addition to your children deriving similar benefits, these activities can help some children with habits such as hand-wringing and nail-biting. They may provide a substitute outlet for these habits.

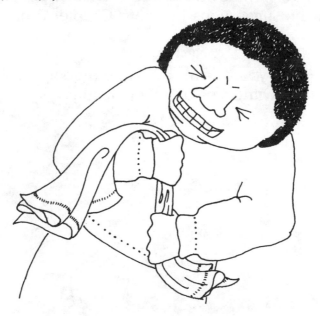

Activity for Kids...

Towel twisting is a way for the hands to release tension. *Towel biting* lets the tension out of the mouth. If you think about it, when you are angry your hands are often in a fist and your jaw is biting down.

So you can let go of this type of steam by:

❦ Twisting a towel as if it is full of water and needs to be wrung out. As you twist the towel it might even help to picture all of the tension draining out of your hands onto the towel. Let the towel become a sponge for the tension in your hands.

❦ If you notice yourself holding in your anger by biting down hard against your own teeth, try biting as hard as you want on a towel instead.

Most people feel less tense in their hands or jaw after doing this activity.

Let Yourself Cry ▪▪▪▪▪▪▪▪▪▪▪▪▪▪▪▪▪▪▪▪▪▪▪▪▪▪▪▪▪

For Parents and Teachers...

Crying is one of the most releasing, relaxing and beneficial expressions of emotion that we have. It is unfortunate that our society discourages this full expression except when an understandable or "reasonable" tragedy occurs. Even then, we tend to applaud those who maintain a "stiff upper lip," perceiving them as emotionally strong.

We often want to "toughen up" our kids, especially boys, so as a society we put out rather clear injunctions against crying at an early age. The result is that many adults develop an unemotional way of dealing with life's stresses that can lead to psychosomatic symptoms (e.g., ulcers, headaches, rashes) which can even be life threatening (heart disease and some cancers have been associated with poor management of stress).

We want to encourage our children to become good problem solvers so that they will feel confident in their skill at dealing with difficult situations. We also want them to know that it is okay to *feel* hurt, upset and sad, and that all people sometimes have these feelings.

A hug, an empathetic ear or arm around the shoulders when tears are flowing tells the child that his tears are both understandable and permissible.

Parents and Teachers Can...

More freely express their range of feelings with their children. I saw the movie *Field of Dreams* with my wife and teenage son. I tried hard to swallow my tears for fear of bursting out crying in the theater when the main character met his deceased father and wanted to "play catch." I felt how I, too, longed for another chance to be with my deceased father.

At the end of the movie, we went to our car and I burst out sobbing as the tears flowed in a steady stream (this is not a usual reaction for me). Through my tears I shared the emptiness of missing my father and how robbed I felt at his not having had a chance to know my children or me as an adult.

Following the display of emotion, my son (not given to emotional expressiveness towards his parents at age 14) gave me a knowing, connected hug. My tears had enriched our relationship.

A few weeks later, still thinking of my father, who had died over 20 years ago, I visited his grave and again began to cry. It felt strangely wonderful to release these belly-driven tears. I left the cemetery with a relaxed calm that I hadn't felt in quite some time.

Activity for Kids...

When you are sad, crying is a wonderful thing to do. So let yourself cry. If you are afraid that others will call you a "sissy," then cry away from them.

Let Yourself Shake ▪▪▪▪▪▪▪▪▪▪▪▪▪▪▪▪▪▪▪▪▪▪▪

For Parents and Teachers...

When we worry a lot, we have little energy to do anything else. Most of us try to think about something else or take a nap or maybe even take some medicine to try to feel better. But sometimes feeling better simply means that we allow our body to do what it wants to do.

Activity for Kids...

The next time you have butterflies racing around in your stomach try this:

1. Instead of trying to make your stomach feel better, let the butterflies or rollercoaster feeling spread from your stomach throughout your body.

2. Your hands, feet, chest, legs, arms and head may feel like shaking because they suddenly have all of this feeling from your stomach. Let any part of your body that wants to shake, do so.

3. Pretty soon your whole body, from the top of your head to the tips of your toes, might feel like shaking. Let your whole body or any of its parts shake until *it* wants to stop.

4. When your body wants to stop shaking, all of the feelings that had been locked inside your stomach will now be all over. You'll feel full of pep and energy. You'll feel excited, not nervous. So do something useful with your excitement.

Write a Letter ▪▪▪▪▪▪▪▪▪▪▪▪▪▪▪▪▪▪▪▪▪▪▪▪▪▪▪▪▪▪▪▪▪

For Parents and Teachers...

Writing can be an extremely effective means for kids to become clear about what they want to say to someone. Writing helps to express feelings that may be harder to say. Perhaps that is why the diary is an outlet used by so many children and adults during their lives.

Other effective modes of creative expression are art, music and drama. You can encourage children to *draw* their feelings, *play or sing* their feelings, or *play-act* or *mime* feelings. A combination of all or some of these modes helps many kids to find effective outlets for their feelings.

Parents and Teachers Can...

Send notes to kids. Teachers can send positive, appreciative notes home that are addressed to a child. Kids feel great when they get a personal note from their teacher. Many kids also respond well to notes that ask for improved behavior.

Sending a note is a private way to ask for something that avoids the embarrassment that kids often feel when they are asked or told in front of their friends. Parents can also leave appreciative notes and those that request improved behavior.

Activity for Kids...

When we have strong feelings toward a person, it may help to write a letter to that person. Just putting down thoughts and feelings on a piece of paper may be a big help in dealing with the strong feelings.

The following is an example of a letter Annie wrote when she was feeling upset at her friend Sarah.

> Dear Sarah,
>
> We've been friends for a long time. It really made me mad when you called me a fat slob. I felt let down because I thought we were good friends. I expect friends to be nicer to me. I still want to be friends but not if you keep calling me names.
>
> Your friend,
>
> Annie

Annie mailed this letter. But a lot of kids who have learned to write these kinds of letters don't mail them. It sometimes helps just to get your feelings down on paper. Then you can decide to send it or not. I've written a lot of letters to people that I never mailed!

Get Good Exercise ▪▪▪▪▪▪▪▪▪▪▪▪▪▪▪▪▪▪▪▪▪▪▪▪▪▪▪▪▪▪

For Parents and Teachers...

Participating in exercise with your child can be a healthy, relaxing, enjoyable way to spend time together. As with other activities in this book, the more you model and/or directly participate in the experience, the more likely is your child to value the activity. When your child observes an active, exercising parent, she is likely to want to join in.

Try to select physical exercise that is fun for both you and your child. Considerable research identifies vigorous exercise as one cause of endorphin release in our brains that makes us feel a natural high. This is usually followed by a fulfilled, relaxing calm.

Activity for Kids...

We can often become more calm and relaxed by exercising properly. Skipping rope, dancing, walking, jogging are all good ways to exercise. Talk to your parents, your doctor or your gym teacher for some ideas that would be right for you.

Don't worry about how you'll look to other people. Taking care of yourself is what's most important. If you're too uptight, pick an exercise that is private. Think of some exercises you like to do. Make a list and post it somewhere to remind yourself to be active.

Eat Right ▪▪▪▪▪▪▪▪▪▪▪▪▪▪▪▪▪▪▪▪▪▪▪▪▪▪▪▪▪▪▪▪▪▪▪▪▪▪▪

For Parents and Teachers...

Research suggests that feelings and behavior are affected by diet and that health and diet are very strongly related. Encourage children to eat foods that are rich in fiber (green and yellow vegetables, fruits and whole grains); calcium (milk and dairy products); iron (dried fruits, *lean* red meat); protein (fish, poultry and lean meat).

Go easy on high fat, high sugar and high salt foods, which can contribute to obesity, high cholesterol, lethargy and hypoglycemia. Note: You may want to define foods as "growing food" and "non-growing" food. The term "junk food" is negative and ambiguous.

Activity for Kids...

A 9-year-old girl named Sue often felt tired even though she got lots of sleep. She also had a lot of bad moods without knowing why. It turned out that Sue ate a lot of food that had sugar and artificial chemicals (cakes, candy bars). She also drank lots of soda and ate almost no fresh fruit, vegetables or whole grains. Sue's behavior and feelings changed when she was put on a healthier diet.

How we feel is caused by lots of different things. But you *may* feel better if you eat more "growing foods," and you *will* be healthier. Talk to your parents, doctor or health teacher for ideas about how you can eat right.

Down the Drain ▪■▪■■▪■■■■▪■■■■■■■■■■■■■■■

For Parents and Teachers...

This activity is similar to the guided picture activities in Chapter 2. If children have been enjoying those activities, they may find this an effective and harmless way to express unpleasant feelings. It is not an activity to be done in regions that are experiencing water shortages, although a bathtub filled for purposes of hygiene can be put to additional use with no more water being used.

All kids who sign their names can have a personal letter written back. Even if kids don't sign their name, it'll help them to know you care, and you can choose to share a "feeling" with the class so that together they might "brainstorm" possible solutions to the problem.

Activity for Kids...

1. Write down all the things you worry about for one week (e.g., pain at the dentist; nobody will want to play with me; I'll get a bad grade on the spelling test).

2. Each time you write down a worry, put it in a shoebox or some other storage box.

3. At the end of the week, read back each of the worries you wrote.

4. Make two piles. One has all the things you worried about that did not actually happen while the other pile has the things that did happen.

Questions:

1. Which pile has more?
2. Was it really worth your time and making yourself tense by imagining all the bad things that could happen?

For all those worries that were wasted try saying the following: "Why was I worried about that? Wasn't it silly for me to waste my time worrying about something out of my control that didn't even happen?"

Worrying about things is okay if there is something that you can actually do to change the situation. For example, worrying that the popular girl in class might not want to play with you provides you with the following choices: (1) I can say nothing and keep worrying; (2) I can ask her to play and she can refuse; (3) I can ask her to play and she can accept.

The first choice is almost always the one that will make you worry the most and the longest because of all the not knowing. You'll keep wondering: should I ask and maybe feel bad if she says no or should I say nothing and hope she notices me. While the second choice isn't pleasant (she doesn't want to play with me), at least you know where she stands so you can stop worrying and start looking for somebody else to play with.

Worry is caused by too much thinking and not enough doing. So take a chance. If you worry a lot, *do* something—be active—get busy—be in charge of your choices—and then worry less!

Chapter 4

Solving Problems and Getting Along with Others

To Parents and Teachers

Some stress-causing problems involve an unsatisfactory relationship that one person has with another. Events such as your boss giving less than an expected raise, a friend who violates your trust by sharing intimate details about you with another, or a spouse who does less around the house than you feel is fair are likely to cause unpleasant stress.

Sulking or screaming, as most of us know, are unlikely to either improve the situation or make us feel better. While imagining a pillow to be the boss (friend, spouse) and pounding or screaming may provide some temporary relief, this type of method will obviously be ineffective in gaining a deserved raise.

This chapter explores concepts and methods that children can use when faced with problems that involve other people. They will learn:

- ❦ How to clearly identify a problem that they have with a parent, teacher, sibling or friend.
- ❦ How to make and evaluate decisions.
- ❦ How to speak up without being either timid or disrespectful.
- ❦ How to be an effective listener.
- ❦ How to avoid being picked on by others, and what to do when this happens.
- ❦ How to get others to be more cooperative and friendly by learning simple principles of positive reinforcement.

The guidance of caring adults in facilitating children's development of these skills is indispensable. The first two activities provide a set of guidelines that help kids learn how to identify and solve problems. While the intent is to focus on interpersonal problems, the same sequence of steps can be effective in addressing a wide range of difficulties.

You are encouraged to become a direct participant in working with children to help guide them through the various problem-solving steps. You can also use this model in seeking solutions to problems that exist within families or classrooms. Just change some of the wording such as, *"What do **you** want to have happen that would make you feel that there is no longer a problem?"* to, *"What do **we** (**each of us**) want in order to correct the problem?"*

Basic psychology teaches us that people are often motivated to seek rewards which are experienced as pleasant. Money, food, vacations and favored activities are the most obvious kinds of rewards. Less obvious, but equally effective, are rewards such as kindness from others, a pat on the back and words of appreciation. Parents, teachers and employers often use a system of rewards to motivate children or employees. They know that behavior which is rewarded is more likely to happen in the future.

So if a child is rewarded for completing classwork by being allowed to go to a special place in the classroom to play a game or to watch a favorite TV show, the child learns to associate work completion with a pleasant consequence. The child will be more likely to repeat this behavior in the future.

Two activities—"Rewarding Others" and "Rewarding Parents and Teachers"—explain this concept to children and show them how they can be more in charge of what happens to them by utilizing these principles with others. As a teacher, you can help a student learn, practice and apply this skill as it pertains to parents and peers. As a parent, you can help your child do likewise with other family members, teachers or peers.

The final activities in this chapter focus on teaching children how to speak up (be assertive) respectfully and how to listen effectively to thoughts and feelings expressed by others. Developing these skills requires *practice*. You can assist by discussing, practicing and role-playing various situations in which these skills may be useful.

To Kids

In this chapter, I hope to give you some good ideas that will help you to solve problems when they come your way. You can be sure that there will be problems. All people have them.

The main difference between people who are successful and those who aren't is in the ability to solve these problems and get along well with other people.

I'm going to show you some very specific steps that you can do that can make you a better problem solver. I'm also going to show you why it's really important to get along as well as you can with powerful grown-ups like parents and teachers.

Even though I know that sometimes a kid just can't influence important grown-ups (like when they have big emotional problems or problems with drugs), lots of other times there are things *you can do* to *make* people treat you better. I want to share some of these ideas with you too.

Finally, I've got some ideas that'll help you stand up and speak out when other kids or grown-ups pick on you. This is called being assertive.

So let's get started. There's lots to learn and practice.

Solving Problems and Getting Along with Others

Solving a Problem ▪▪▪▪▪▪▪▪▪▪▪▪▪▪▪▪▪▪▪▪▪▪▪▪▪▪▪

For Parents and Teachers...

Some problems we have can be solved, while others can only be accepted. For example, if a child has a problem making friends, that can usually be solved. But if the problem is that the child's parents are planning to divorce, there is probably nothing that a child can do to stop it.

Finding solutions even to problems that can be solved can be difficult, but there are specific steps that can be identified. Children can learn these steps and apply them to problems over which they have some control.

Parents and Teachers Can...

Assist children in identification and application of the steps for problem solving. Being clear on what the problem is can be difficult for adults, let alone children. We can help children both in the process of applying the steps to their own problems and by modeling the steps when addressing problems we face.

Activity for Kids...

It is important to know the difference between problems that you can solve and problems you can't. It's not always easy to tell the difference, because often there are some things you can control and some things you can't. For example, you can't control which teacher you are assigned.

Some problems can be completely controlled (doing my arithmetic assignment; deciding to say yes or no to drugs) and some can't be controlled by you at all (my father's drinking problem; my parents' decision to divorce; the neighborhood I live in).

For the problems and parts of problems you can solve, the following steps have been useful to many people:

Step 1. You must first know exactly what the problem is. Saying that the problem is "Dad gets on my case" is not specific enough. Saying that "Dad yells at me when he thinks I haven't done my chores" is specific.

Step 2. You must know what you want to have happen. (What is your goal?) "I want Dad to tell me when he is angry instead of yelling at me." (This is like "setting a goal" in Chapter 1.)

Step 3. With a friend, a bunch of friends, a teacher who understands or even with Dad, think about all the solutions that might solve this problem. Write down all the solutions, even if some seem silly.
I can do my chores all the time.
I can ask Dad to talk softly rather than yell.
I can yell back.
I can pack my bags and leave home.
I can tell Dad that it upsets me when he yells.

Step 4. Cross out all the solutions on your list that could not possibly solve this problem.

Step 5. Pick one of the solutions to try that you think would be a good one and do it.

Step 6. If that solution doesn't work, either pick another one or do the whole thing again with other people.

Step 7. If the problem continues after four attempts to solve it by using these steps, you might have to accept that the problem may not be able to be solved with the person. But before you give up, talk to a *helping person* like a counselor, a psychologist or a teacher. Even when problems can't be solved, people can learn how to accept them without getting so upset and feeling guilty. When problems you can't control won't go away it still feels good to share your worries with someone who cares. You are not alone! There are people who can help.

Problem-Solving Review for Kids:

1. What is the problem?
   The problem is_____.

2. What do you want to have happen that would make you feel that there is no longer a problem?
   I want_____. Or, my goal is_____.

3. List all possible solutions (even silly ones).

4. Judge each of the possible solutions. Cross out those that you don't think would work.

5. Pick one of the solutions that you think might work and try it.

6. Pick another solution if the first one doesn't make the problem better or do steps one through five again.

7. Talk to someone about the problem when you run out of solutions.

Mutual Problem Solving ▪▪▪▬▬▬▬▬▬▬▬▬▬▬▬▬

For Parents and Teachers...

There are times when parents and teachers need to assert their demands without regard to reaching a consensus agreement. For example, we would consider it preposterous to take a vote among 3 year olds as to how many think they should look both ways before crossing the street. On certain issues, especially those with a safety factor, we want to firmly *tell and show* children what to do, *not* negotiate a compromise.

However, in the long term, the goal is for our children to become good, capable decision makers. And there is no better way than for the family or classroom to become an alive, exciting place where problems are greeted as an opportunity for people to practice and refine their decision-making, problem-solving skills.

Undone chores, incomplete homework, a stolen book, a messy room and tattling become the opportunities to further our children's skills at becoming better decision makers. When we are frustrated, sharing these frustrations with our children can be a good opener for having us all put our heads together to come up with a helpful solution.

As a parent, I have found that at least weekly family council meetings with all family members present for about one hour can be very useful in sharing appreciations with each other, as well as in identifying problems and their solutions.

Classroom meetings at school can serve the same purpose. Instead of lecturing and insisting, during a classroom meeting the teacher says, "Paints and brushes were not put away, which created a mess on the floor. Our two problems are: (1) cleaning up the mess, and (2) making a plan so that the problem doesn't happen again. Any ideas?" The teacher (parents) can then use the seven problem-solving steps to help the class (child) solve the problem.

This type of mutual problem-solving builds a cooperative bond. It also sends a strong message of respect to children—I believe in your ability to actively participate in a meaningful way to help solve problems and make this a better place. That is a very positive way to communicate trust and build competence.

Parents and Teachers Can...

Use problem solving in efforts to resolve lots of sticky situations. Faber and Mazlish, in their book *How to Talk so Kids Will Listen and How to Listen so Kids Will Talk* (Avon Books, 1980), describe a 5-step problem-solving method:

1. Talk about the child's feelings and needs. ("It's probably not easy to remember to do your chores when your friends are knocking on the door and want you to play.")

2. Talk about your feelings and needs. ("On the other hand, when the house is a mess, that creates more work for me.")

3. Brainstorm to find a mutually agreeable solution. ("Let's put our heads together and come up with some ideas that would be good for us.")

4. Write down all ideas without evaluating.

5. Decide which you like, which you don't like and which you plan to follow through (all people in the conflict do this together).

Rewarding (Stroking) Others

For Parents and Teachers...

In his classic book *Between Parent and Child* Ginott (MacMillan, 1970), Dr. Haim Ginott distinguishes between feedback that is evaluative and feedback that is appreciative.

Evaluative feedback places one person in the role of judge and the other as the one being judged. Appreciative feedback is when one person tells another how he was affected by what the other person did.

Feedback such as "I loved listening to your piano playing" is appreciative. Telling someone that they're great is evaluative. Evaluative feedback often starts with "you" while appreciative feedback starts with "I." Most people prefer feeling appreciated, not judged.

Parents and Teachers Can...

Practice using I-statements in dealing with others. (See Chapter 2 for more information on I-statements.) The more you practice, the more routine it becomes. You then serve as a powerful model for children and other adults regarding interpersonal relations.

Activity for Kids...

One way to make yourself be more in charge is by learning how to reward other people. Parents and teachers use rewards a lot to get kids to behave. Getting a sticker or a high grade in school is a kind of reward. Being paid for mowing the lawn is a reward. Being told that you did a good job or being given a candy bar for being kind to your little sister or brother are other kinds of rewards.

In order for a reward to be really effective, we must truly mean it when we give it. It's got to come from the heart. And while that may sound tough to do, most of the time it's pretty easy.

All we have to do is notice the positive things we like that other people do, tell them and ignore the things they do that we don't like. Think about it, don't you like it when other people notice the positive things *you* do? Doesn't it usually make you want to do more of those things?

A reward is a positive way that people notice each other. Rewards can be positive *words* (saying thank you; wow—that was really great!), *actions* (being a helper; doing something because you know it'll please somebody else), or *things* (buying a candy bar for someone; a friendly note to someone; a gift).

Sometimes a parent might reward a kid with an extra *privilege* like watching more TV or staying up late if he behaves responsibly. But the main rewards that kids can share are *words*, *actions* and *things*.

It is amazing to see how hard people (grown-ups too) will work to keep getting rewards or *strokes*. By the way, a stroke is just another way to talk about what happens between people when they communicate. Good strokes are words, actions or things that make us feel appreciated, important or special. Bad strokes are words, actions or things that hurt our feelings or make us upset.

One thing to know is that *all* people need strokes. If we don't get good ones, then we'll work to get bad ones. Failing in school, starting fights or saying mean things are ways that some people get negative attention or strokes. Nobody wants to be ignored, so if we don't get good strokes then bad ones are better than none at all.

When you learn to give other people good or positive strokes, you'll see that they will want to give you good ones in return (most of the time).

So if you want others to treat you well, you must first treat them well. This can be hard for some of us to do at first, but it's really pretty easy to learn.

All you have to do is be a good guesser. That's right! Your job is to figure out what it is that another person finds rewarding. And that's easier than you might think. Down below, we'll help you figure out ways to reward or give positive strokes to other kids. The next activity will show you how to reward or stroke teachers and parents.

Step 1. Think about the kinds of rewards and strokes that you like. Make a list of three and share the list with a parent or teacher or friend. Maybe the rewards are the same as those you wrote in "Reward Yourself," Chapter 1. Maybe there are others that come to mind. What are they?

Step 2. Think about a kid you'd like to get friendlier with. What are some words, actions or things that he finds rewarding? If you don't know, ask. But probably when that kid laughs, smiles or is having a good time, he is feeling rewarded. When are such times? Look and observe.

Step 3. Think of what you might say or do that would feel good to you *and* also be one of the things you noticed the other kid likes.

Step 4. Do it! Take a chance!! The worst that can happen is that this other kid won't appreciate you or want to be friends. Even "good" rewarders can't win them all.

Rewarding Teachers and Parents■■■

For Parents and Teachers...

You may hear your child complain about a mean teacher, nasty friend, nagging sister or annoying relative. You can introduce the idea suggested above by helping her identify ways in which these people might be rewarded and how that would be good for her.

Use the following questions as a guide:

1. Why do you think _____ does or says _____ to you?

2. What kind of behavior do you think _____ wants from you?

3. Let's try to put ourselves in _____ shoes. As this person, let's think about what we like and what we don't like.

4. Now that we've guessed these things, do you have any ideas about what you can choose to do to get along better with _____?

5. Will you do this new thing with _____ for one week? Then let's talk again next week and see how things are going.

Parents and Teachers Can...

Actively show children that they have more power to influence the behavior of others than they might think. Most kids who have trouble getting along have relatively poor social skills. They don't make eye contact when they speak. Using "please," "thank you" and other social graces is not a standard part of their repertoire. They don't know how to show a level of interest nor have they mastered the power of the smile.

These kids need you to tell them, show them and most importantly, they need a chance to practice these behaviors with someone they can trust. Then they can go into the "real" world and see how effective they have become.

I am reminded of Luis, a 10-year-old withdrawn, angry boy who often felt picked on by adults with authority. His fourth grade teacher had a lot of trouble managing his behavior, and frequent phone calls home, threats and detentions were used unsuccessfully. I asked Luis to be a "scientist" for one week by experimenting with new behavior to see if he could get his teacher "off his case."

Luis practiced looking his teacher in the eyes in a friendly way and saying, "Hello Mr. _____." He also agreed to give two compliments to his teacher each day, beginning with the words "I liked or enjoyed it when _____." Luis seemed very pleased to notice some positive changes in his teacher. He was able to directly see the connection between his actions and their effects on a powerful other.

Although Luis hasn't become a model student, he has learned to take more responsibility for causing what happens to him. Discuss the example below. Before you tell the child(ren) what can be done, invite them to offer their own ideas. You can give other examples as well.

Activity for Kids...

Steve has been having trouble getting along with his music teacher because sometimes he finds music boring. He decides to fool around in class, make noises and constantly drop his books on the floor to disturb the class.

How do you think the music teacher is going to feel about Steve? Right! She's going to think of him as disrespectful and rude. She may threaten to call his parents and send him to the principal's office.

Now Steve decides that he doesn't want the music teacher on his case. What can he do?

1. He guesses that his teacher likes music because she teaches it.

2. He asks himself to figure out what most teachers find rewarding. That's pretty easy to do:

- ❦ Teachers like kids who participate in class by asking a question or giving an answer. Steve can raise his hand and ask a question about music.
- ❦ Teachers like kids who are polite. Steve could thank her after class for today's lesson or tell her about something he learned in class today that he found interesting. Most teachers find it very rewarding to be appreciated by their students.
- ❦ Teachers like kids who show interest in class. Steve could show his interest by making good eye contact with the teacher. He could also nod his head up and down occasionally to show that he is really interested.
- ❦ Teachers like kids who get good grades. That makes teachers feel that they have really taught a kid something. Steve could work harder and get better grades, or at least put forth more effort.

Now, Steve doesn't have to do all of these things. But if he did at least a few of them, he and his teacher would probably have a better relationship.

You can do the same kinds of things with your parents or other people. You can get them to be nice to you most of the time. Try to figure out what they find rewarding and give them that.

- Thank Dad once in a while for working hard to support the family.
- Tell Mom how much you appreciate the things she does for you.
- Say hello to a teacher you don't like, with a smile on your face.
- Buy your little sister a treat once in awhile after she hasn't given you a hard time.
- Do a chore before you're reminded to do so.

Notice how people will begin to appreciate you more when you are interested and courteous. And when people are nicer to you, there is less stress in life.

What do you think your parent(s) finds rewarding?

What do you think your teacher finds rewarding?

Making Friends with Your Enemy━━━

For Parents and Teachers...

Kids need to learn how to stand up in an assertive way when either verbally or physically attacked by peers. But of even greater importance is that they maintain their own dignity by continuing to reach out to others with an arm of friendship.

A teacher friend of mine stated that in his school children are taught that kids who act mean and call other kids names are really feeling bad inside and that they need others to help them feel good. So all the kids practice how to say positive things when they hear put-downs.

For example, if one child says condescendingly to another, "You buck-tooth-ugly-mouth!," the "victim" is likely to answer, "You're right—I have buck teeth—but your teeth are beautiful!" With practice, many kids found both a way to avoid fights and say positive things.

Parents and Teachers Can...

Use questions similar to those in the activity to stimulate discussions about this theme. You might also offer some of your own experiences to children about ways that you became friends with people who at first gave you a hard time.

Better yet, if you continue to hold a grudge with someone, you can actually demonstrate the concept of this activity by letting go of your resentment and doing something to end hostilities. Remember, kids learn according to how they see trusted others behave.

Activity for Kids...

David, a 9-year-old boy, was climbing a tree one day to get into a tree fort built by Jason. By accident he slipped and fell. Even though he got only a few bumps and bruises, he became very angry, lost his temper and broke the tree fort to pieces. Jason got so mad that he wrecked David's bike to get even. They became enemies until about a week later when Jason offered to help fix David's bike if David would help to rebuild the fort. They both agreed and became friends again.

You may also be able to turn an enemy into a friend.

Questions:

1. Think about somebody that you don't get along with.

2. Why do you think there is a problem? (Lots of times another kid may be mean to you because she is jealous or because she wishes she were as popular, smart or attractive as you are.)

3. What do you think might happen if you did something first to try to make this person into a friend? (It sometimes works to offer this kid help with her work, to invite her to go to a movie, to make sure to say hello every day, to ask her in private if she has problems that she'd like to talk about, to do a project of some kind with her.)

4. What do you think *you* will choose to do to try to make this enemy into a friend?

Aggressive-Passive-Assertive ▪■▪■■▪▪▪▪▪▪▪▪▪

For Parents and Teachers...

When we shout or yell at someone, use our fists to solve problems or attack people with put-downs or nasty words, that is being *aggressive*. Aggressive people don't solve problems, they only create more problems.

Another way to solve problems with people is to make believe they don't exist and to do nothing. Adults and kids who solve problems this way are *passive*. They may feel hurt, angry, upset or sad, but never let anybody know when they are bothered.

They keep it all inside because they worry that if they stand up for their rights, even worse things will happen. But doing nothing when other people bug you doesn't make problems go away.

Assertive kids and adults stand up for their rights without getting into fights. They talk straight, but they don't put others down. They look at other people when they talk, and they say their words with feeling. They look and sound confident. They use I-statements (Chapter 2) to say what they want and how they feel.

Parents and Teachers Can...

Work with children to evaluate each of these situations (numbers 2 and 5 show an assertive response). Discuss the probable outcomes to each of the examples. It helps to ask, "What do you think would happen next if _____ did that? Do you think that would be a good solution or a bad solution?"

You can also use the examples to stimulate thinking about how the kids who acted passively or aggressively could have been assertive.

Finally, you might want to identify specific troublesome situations currently faced by your child in his relationships with others and assist him in developing and practicing an assertive response.

Some kids with very poor self-esteem have developed a sense of confidence about themselves through training in the martial arts. Confidence in oneself is necessary in order for kids to see themselves as worthy enough to stand up for themselves in a dignified, confident manner.

Taking every opportunity that you can find to notice and reinforce your child's competence and success will also help him/her to become an assured person.

Activity for Kids...

Many people don't do a very good job when it comes to speaking up for their rights. When they feel upset or frustrated they yell, shout, hit or swear. These people are *aggressive*. Although they may solve the immediate problem, in the long run their behavior makes other people angry and want to attack back.

Aggressive people actually create problems for other people and for themselves. Do you know any aggressive people? How do you feel when you are around them?

Another way to solve problems is to make believe they don't exist and hope they go away. People who are *passive* act as if they had no rights at all. They do nothing when picked on, put-down or pushed away. Do you know people who often act in a passive way? How do you think they feel?

Sometimes it may be wise to act aggressive or passive. For example, if someone is attacking you with fists you may have no choice but to fight back and protect yourself (aggressive). If a gang of kids is calling you names, even though you feel mad, it's probably best to keep on walking and say nothing (passive). Your health should be more important than your pride.

The good news is that there is a third way to behave which is called being *assertive*. Kids who are assertive talk straight but they don't put others down. They look at other people when they talk and they say their words with feeling. They look and sound confident. They also use I-statements to tell how they feel.

There are almost always *four* assertive things you can say when you need to stand up for your rights. Here's how it might work.

Steve's little brother just took a toy that belongs to Steve. Steve first says, "Please give me my truck back." If his brother refuses, he next says slowly with good eye contact, "I'm asking you to give me my truck back."

If his brother still refuses, the third step is to say firmly, "I'm telling you to give me my truck back." Finally, if Steve's brother still refuses he ends by saying, "Either give me my truck back now or I'll tell Mom and she'll get it back for me."

To review, use I-statements to tell what you want and how you feel (assertive). You can just about always use four steps (the "four-step"):

Step 1: Use "Please" when asking for what you want.
Step 2: Start by saying, "I'm asking you to _____."
Step 3: Say firmly, "I'm telling you that I _____."
Step 4: Say what you'll do if the person still refuses. "Last chance before I tell Mom (Dad, Teacher), who I know will help."

Practice it. Get good at it. You can become assertive.

Situations:

Now that you have learned the differences between *aggressive*, *passive* and *assertive* behavior, decide which type of response is being shown by each of the main characters in the following:

1. Steve says, "You're a stupid, fat, ugly geek."

2. Micky finds out that a group of buddies is going to the movies and they didn't invite him. He calls and says, "I feel hurt and angry that you didn't invite me to the movies. I don't understand why I was left out."

3. George's father accuses him of breaking one of his tools, even though George didn't. George hangs his head and walks away.

4. Lois puts down Mary's mother. Mary punches her in the face.

5. Julie's teacher gives her a lower grade on her essay than she thinks she deserves. Julie says, "Mrs. Smith, when you gave me a C, I felt disappointed and upset. I put out a lot of effort and thought I deserved a higher grade. I don't understand your thinking. Would you please explain?"

Questions:

1. Can you think of someone who recently took something that belonged to you?
2. How might you use the four steps to get it back? Practice.

3. Can you think of someone who keeps saying or doing things to hurt your feelings?

4. Have you tried to really ignore the person who does this (pretend he doesn't really exist)?

5. If you've ignored it and you keep getting bugged, try "the four-step." Practice it with a friend or parent before you actually do it.

Chapter 5

Special Problems

To Parents and Teachers

Some children are faced with extremely difficult situations or problems that make them feel helpless and out-of-control. This brief final chapter identifies some of these major problems and provides support, encouragement and direction for children who are experiencing these unfortunate life crises.

It is beyond the scope of this book to address these very complex problems in detail. I present them mainly in an effort to heighten your awareness and that of your children and to provide some basic suggestions that let kids and families know that help for these problems is available.

Parents and teachers need to be well informed about the availability of community resources that address the problems of children and their families. There is never any shame in seeking help for problems which seem overwhelming. Most communities offer support groups and counseling services. Take advantage of these resources.

If you are a parent and don't know where to begin, start with your child's pediatrician, teacher or school mental health professional. Describe the problem that you suspect your child or family has and ask for a referral to an appropriate agency or professional who is well-trained to handle the problem you describe.

It is never too late to provide appropriate support for your child and for yourself!

To Kids

Kids feel the most stress when there are important, negative things that are happening which they just don't think they can control. *Big* problems that some kids face are: parents getting divorced; divorced parents who hate each other and talk to you about it; living with a disabled or sick relative; using drugs or living with a relative who does; being hit; being touched in your private places.

If any of these things are happening to you, I hope that you will see that there is help available to you. I'll share some ideas about what to do and whom you can see for more help. Read on!

Divorce ▪▪

For Parents and Teachers...

Nearly one in two marriages ends in divorce. Many remarry, thereby creating blended families. Only about half of all children who are born today will be living with both biological parents by the time they complete high school. This suggests that many kids can personally identify with divorce and its effects because they have been through it.

No matter how bad the marriage, divorce is rarely easy for anyone. Younger kids may feel they have caused the problems. They need much reassurance. They need to be told clearly and directly: "This is not your fault. Kids *never* cause divorce. We have grown-up problems and we need to be apart."

Divorce is a tumultuous time for all. It is difficult to predict all the changes that are likely. But the clearer you can be with your children, the better they will be.

They need to know:

> Where will I be living?
> With whom will I be living?
> Will I get to see Dad (Mom) and how often?
> Does everyone still love me?
> What will we do during holidays?
> Did I do something wrong to cause these problems?
> Will I still be able to go to school with my friends?

The divorces that seem to impact children the least negatively are those in which parents are able to avoid the trap of involving kids in the middle of the conflict where they are forced to choose sides. Even though you (parent) are no doubt upset, frustrated and angry, there will be a better long-term outcome if you can protect both your and your ex-spouse's dignity by refusing the temptation to get your child on your side. Your child loves you and is on the side of doing the best he can do to cope with a difficult situation.

For Kids...

When parents get divorced, it is a sad and scary time for most kids. Most kids wonder if they caused it, and many try hard to do everything possible to keep their parents together. Even after the divorce, many kids still keep hoping and trying to get their parents back together.

Divorce changes your life. It affects where you live, how often you can see a parent, where you go to school and which friends you'll still be around.

These changes are very hard. *First,* you must not blame yourself. Grown-ups get divorced because they are unhappy with each other. No matter how good or bad you behaved, that is *never* the reason for the divorce, even if you overhear your parents arguing about the kids. Probably they argued or disagreed about lots of things, which is why they are divorcing.

Second, it is understandable that you feel upset, sad, worried, angry, confused or all of these.

Third, it can help to talk with other kids whose parents have divorced and grown-ups, such as counselors and teachers, who can understand.

Finally, I'd like to recommend a few books for you and your parents that will help. You'll find most of these books at the end of this chapter.

Blended Families ▪▪▪▪▪▪▪▪▪▪▪▪▪▪▪▪▪▪▪▪▪▪▪▪▪▪▪▪▪▪▪

For Parents, Teachers and Kids...

Approximately one child in four is a stepchild. Most stepparents don't realize it until they are living it, but the blended family is a much more complex set of emotional relationships than the biological family. There are many people involved.

The feelings of a natural mother or father toward a child are different than they are toward a stepchild. The feelings of a stepchild toward a natural parent are different from her feelings toward a stepparent.

Virtually all feelings and issues that exist in biological families are heightened in blended families. For example, jealousy naturally occurs in biological families (siblings jealous of each other or a parent jealous of attention given to a child by a spouse). But in blended families, everybody is forever checking to see if someone is paying more attention to someone else.

Blended families are also loaded with ambivalent feelings. The fact is that at best there is a mix of caring, along with anger and resentment, felt by all. Everybody had prior relationships that are threatened by the new family.

A son worries about being replaced by a stepfather. A daughter feels disloyal to her dead father if she bonds with a stepfather. Who is this "stranger" ordering me around? wonders nine-year-old Sally. Lee, age six, feels angry that her stepsister Joyce's grandparents gave Joyce a Christmas present but not her. In short, living in a blended family is very difficult and challenging for all.

Blended families should establish at least weekly family meetings where all are present and time is given for the sharing of gripes, problems and appreciations. The setting aside of time in this format will help establish a sense of unity.

As a stepparent, be prepared to do a lot of nonjudgmental listening. Use I-statements to convey your wants and needs to your stepchildren and encourage them to do the same. Reach out to establish some emotional bonding.

As a family, you can use the problem-solving steps outlined in this book during family meetings when problems arise. Many other activities in this book can help in building positive relationships between family members. For more information, see the Resources page at the end of the book.

Abuse ▪▪

For Parents and Teachers...

Sometimes our kids need protection from adults with problems. Often, these are the people who are supposed to love them the most. Abused children will *always* have problems unless they and their families receive proper treatment. The emphasis in most communities is therefore upon treatment rather than punishment. Dealing with abuse is *never* pleasant but *always* necessary.

If you know or suspect that your child is being physically or sexually abused by another family member you **must** not allow this to continue. It is only by reporting to the proper authorities that intervention and treatment can take place. Most communities have abuse hotlines from which you can get the information you need to help a child in distress.

For Kids...

Some of us unfortunately live with parents, grandparents or other family members who can't, won't, or don't want to care for us properly. Some kids live with parents who need to call them *stupid, fat, ugly* or *useless.* Even worse, some kids have been or are being punched, kicked, hit or sexually touched (touched in private places) by people who are supposed to love them.

Unfortunately, there are some grown-ups who are so unhappy, and have such big problems, that they take out their misery on the people who are closest to them—their kids.

Don't allow anybody, even people you love, to hit you over and over. No one should touch you in your private body places either. I know it is very scary to tell somebody when this is happening because you are not sure who you can trust. You might be afraid that you won't be believed, and you are scared that you'll get hit or touched worse if the person finds out you have told.

Please take a chance. You need help and so does the person who is hurting you.

Tell either your teacher, school nurse, psychologist, guidance counselor or social worker. Even though all kids are afraid to share these "secrets," there just isn't any other way to get help for yourself and for the people who are hurting you.

The *helping people* know how to make sure that you will be protected. They are trained to know what to do when these bad things happen to kids.

Illness ▪▪

For Parents and Teachers...

In most cities across the country, there are programs and services offered to families who are struggling with the situation of having a loved one with an acute or chronic illness or disability. These families not only struggle to cope with the physical care that is required, but often family members have feelings of resentment, fear or anger that cause distress.

It is not necessary for symptoms of distress to be apparent in order for children (or adults) to benefit from being in a support group with others who are experiencing similar circumstances. For example, I run a monthly support group in collaboration with Ms. Jody Atkin in Rochester, NY, for children ages 7-14 who have physically or intellectually disabled brothers and sisters.

We have found the vast majority of these children to be well-adjusted. However, they love coming to group because it is there that they find others who have some of the same unique issues that sometimes make coping difficult.

You need to know your community's resources in order to seek this kind of support. A call to your local United Way is a good place to start. Many hospitals offer social work services to families that are trying to adjust to life with a sick or disabled family member.

For Kids...

Some of us live with a very sick relative, which can make life very tough. A brother who may die from cancer, a sister who can't walk or talk, a father with a weak heart or a sick mother all require extra care.

It is very normal for you to feel sad and worried in situations such as these. It is also normal to feel angry about all the extra attention or care that is needed by the sick or disabled person, which means there is less attention for you. Remember, all of your feelings are okay.

Many of the activities in this book can help you feel calmer and more relaxed, and some can help you solve some of your problems. It may also help to talk to someone who can understand what you are going through. Other kids who are going through the same things, a close friend, a counseling center or the hospital are good places to get the help and caring you need. Your school probably has a social worker or a guidance counselor who is trained to be a good listener. Your church minister can also help. Pick whomever you want.

Just realize that you don't have to be alone with your feelings.

Death ■■

For Parents and Teachers...

When kids experience the death of a relative or friend, it is quite natural for them both to mourn for the departed or departing loved one and to worry about their own security. They often wonder who will care for them.

Addressing these concerns In an upfront, forthright manner by acknowledging your own mortality and specifying who will care for your kids in the event of your absence can be quite reassuring. Perhaps the greatest tragedy is when another child, relative or friend, dies. Such tragedies tear away at us, often leading us to question the very values and beliefs by which we live.

When kids lose a friend or relative, they may question the very meaning of life. Why did this happen? How could this happen? Why would God make this happen?

During the period of asking questions with no easy answers, children will also feel grief. They may begin by denying their feelings because they are so overwhelmed.

During this phase, they may appear outwardly calm, seemingly unfazed by it all. In a sense, they are in shock. This can be quickly followed by depression (sadness, emptiness, loneliness) and anger.

Only after experiencing the feelings, preferably in the company of others who feel similarly, does the process of accepting the loss begin. This can take many months. Providing emotional support by being there as a loving, concerned adult can be reassuring.

It is generally advisable to permit even young children to attend the wake, services and the funeral. Be guided by your child's questions and his expressed need to participate.

Older children might want to get together and decide on a way to memorialize a friend. This is an important part of the healing process.

If signs of depression persist beyond a few weeks, then contact your pediatrician or a mental health professional.

For Kids...

When we lose someone we love forever through death, it is okay to feel very scared, sad, angry and even down in the dumps. The first thing to remember is that death is *never* your fault.

It is normal for all kids to sometimes wish that a parent or a teacher or a sibling was dead (especially when they do things that make you mad). But wishing doesn't make things happen. If it did, then I would have been a millionaire years ago.

When we wish for something bad and then that bad thing happens, we may feel very guilty because we think that the bad wish made the bad thing happen. Then we blame ourselves, thinking that it was all our fault. You must remember that the bad thing happening and the wish have nothing to do with each other.

Sometimes a friend or a family member dies. When that happens it seems almost impossible to believe. It is hard to understand that someone we knew and loved will never be with us again. That makes us feel very sad and empty and causes most of us to cry.

We also feel helpless because there is nothing we can do to bring this person back. Losing someone we love *always* makes us want to ask questions. You have every right to ask and keep asking until you get an answer or until you are satisfied that there isn't one. Ask your mom and dad. Ask your priest or rabbi. Ask your teacher or school counselor.

Share your thoughts, ideas and feelings with friends, especially those who also knew the person that died. Let yourself cry or be angry.

If your friend's death causes you to worry about your own death, remember that most kids live to be old people, probably you will too, but it is okay to feel afraid of dying. Most people are. You need to talk about that.

Finally, it might help you to feel better if you planned to do something with others that would keep the memory of your friend or family member alive.

Drugs and Alcohol ▬▬▬▬▬▬▬▬▬▬▬▬▬▬▬

For Parents and Teachers...

Get involved in gaining thorough information about drug abuse prevention. Join a community group that is active in promoting drug-free fun for kids. There are an increasing number of communities that have groups in which parents sign a roster to indicate that their home is drug-free and adult-supervised during parties.

If you suspect that your child is using drugs, you can generally enlist the cooperation of your child's physician, school personnel and a drug rehabilitation center in seeking proper guidance. Most schools have a drug abuse professional on staff.

Kids who abuse drugs will use whatever methods necessary, including lying and deceit, to continue their habit. You must not be afraid to use assertive and if necessary coercive means to rescue your child from his self-destructive behavior.

Drug and alcohol use is a serious adult problem. Kids who live with a chemically dependent parent are subject to severe stress due to the unpredictability and unreliability of parents with this problem.

Such children question their own abilities, often feel to blame for the parent's problem, worry about injury or damage to property, feel helpless, are embarrassed to bring friends home and then feel guilty about being ashamed.

A friend of mine who is a drug abuse coordinator in a suburban school district recently told me that she estimates that in a regular elementary school class of 25 children, there are 5 who live with the effects of alcohol and other drug abuse on a daily basis.

As a teacher, I suggest that you invite drug professionals into the class who can stimulate discussion and let both you and the children know where to get help and how to access it.

If you are a nonchemically dependent parent who is living with a chemically dependent spouse, your child's mental health and well-being (as well as your own) depends upon your contact with the competent help that is available. If you don't know where to begin, call the nearest Alcoholics Anonymous.

As the parent or teacher of a child ten years old or younger, your efforts are best geared toward prevention. All children need to feel that they are worthwhile, liked by and important to someone who is important to them. They need to succeed at important tasks that are reinforced by their environment, and they need to feel that they have the power to influence the environment in which they live.

Children who feel good view themselves as important to others, capable of successfully meeting challenging tasks and mostly in control of themselves and the world around them. They achieve a natural high when they are class helper or monitor because they feel affirmed. They feel good when they can use and enhance their power by making decisions that affect their lives.

Children who seem to be bored, inattentive, daydreaming, poor achievers in school or lacking friends are receiving negative messages from their environment and may begin to feel inadequate, incapable and incomplete. Drug prevention really means bolstering and boosting self-esteem, so that the child views himself as being effective in this world rather than needing chemical relief from life's pressures. Many of the activities (especially in Chapter 1) are designed to help kids learn to feel good about themselves.

For Kids...

If it hasn't happened yet, you can be sure that some day another kid will offer you drugs. Many kids try drugs and alcohol because they are curious about how drugs make them feel and because they are afraid that their friends won't like them unless they join the crowd.

My advice is simple. Unless a doctor gives you drugs because you are sick, don't take them! Sometimes it is best to keep on being curious rather than risk doing something that is very dangerous.

I can be curious about how it would feel to go over a giant waterfall in a barrel, but if I do it, chances are very good that I won't live to tell about it. And if other kids won't be your friends unless you do drugs, then they don't care about you anyway.

You've got to care about and love yourself. Find other friends. Some older kids I've worked with who used to do drugs tell me that the breathing and picture activities in this book really work to get them relaxed. These are safe ways to handle stress, instead of the dangerous escape of drugs.

If one of your parents has a problem with drugs or alcohol, then that's probably causing you a lot of troubles. Parents with drug problems might act unpredictably—you're never sure what mood they're in. You probably feel embarrassed to invite a friend over because of the way your parent might act if drunk or high.

You might even think you are to blame for the problem, because people on drugs usually blame everyone except themselves for their problems. You probably worry a lot about your parent and probably try to do everything you can to keep things perfect. Maybe you've even gotten disgusted and mad.

Maybe you can't concentrate in school and you don't think anyone can understand. Well, you are wrong! If you look around your class there are probably 3 or 4 other kids dealing with the same problem who are just as uncomfortable as you are to share that. That is why there are people at school (drug abuse professionals) or people in the community who can help.

If you don't know where else to turn, look up Alcoholics Anonymous in the phone book and call. You'll find more references on the Resources page at the end of the book.

When to Seek Professional Help ■■■■■■■■■■■■■■■■■■■■■■■■■

For Parents and Teachers...

There are times when a child's thoughts, feelings or behaviors require professional help. Parents must put aside pride or concern about appearances. Children are sometimes overwhelmed by stress. Among the *alert signs* that signal the need for professional help are:

❦ Changes in sleep and/or eating habits, which may signal underlying depression.
❦ Speech that contains content such as "I wish I were dead," or "I have nothing to live for."
❦ An increasing withdrawal from others, becoming emotionally isolated.
❦ Giving away of personal possessions, particularly those with personal or sentimental value.

- Self-injurious behavior, such as carving marks on any part of the body.
- A chronic sense of worry and negativism about oneself and/or others.
- A sudden uplifting of spirits in which the youth seems to have finally "broken out" of a depression.
- Frequent aggressive behavior which may result in injury to others or damage to property.
- Deliberate physical cruelty to animals.
- Fire-setting, frequent lying or stealing.
- Poor adjustment at school.

For Kids...

It is sad and tragic that some young people feel so depressed about their problems that they see no way out but to hurt themselves or others. Not eating, difficulty sleeping, getting down on yourself, worrying, hurting animals, getting into many fights, doing poorly at school, lying or stealing a lot are all signs that you are in trouble and need help.

The good news is that there are a lot of people who know how to help when you are very stressed out. But you must have the courage to share these thoughts and feelings with a trained person. If you have tried to tell a friend or a parent about your unhappiness but they just don't seem to understand, don't give up.

Every city, town and village has a hospital with help available. And many places have a *hotline* that you can call to speak with someone who will steer you to the right place for the kind of help you need.

Many people experience problems in their lives that seem so huge that there just doesn't seem to be any way out. That's why it is so important for you to seek help. A solution to your problem may be as simple as some medicine that will make you feel better. Lately it's been found that a lot of people who get depressed are helped by certain medicines or changes in their diet.

The best medicine is usually just being with people who understand, who can listen and who care!

Final Thoughts
for Parents and Teachers ■■■■■■■IIIIIIIIIIIIIIIIIII

As parents and teachers we need to teach our children to cope with life's situations. We live in a fast-paced, always changing world. We need to provide them with a solid foundation that enables them to understand their mistakes, learn from them and go on with their lives.

There is no ready-made formula by which we do this. We need to realize that all children need to be loved, respected and thought of as terrific by at least one other human being in order for them to develop a positive view of themselves.

You can be that person for your child or as a teacher, for one or more of those children who don't get it at home.

This book has emphasized the importance of loving adults who show understanding, are available to listen in times of crisis, give support, encourage problem-solving, share their ideas and listen without criticism.

I have included several other references on the Resource page from which you can obtain more information on the topics covered in this book.

The future of our world depends upon today's children becoming tomorrow's compassionate adults.

Final Thoughts for Kids ━━━━━━━━━━━━━━

Maybe you've heard grown-ups tell you to enjoy being a kid because these are the best years of your life! For many kids who have parents that love them, who have a lot of friends, are smart at school, who are good looking and who have discovered how to feel good about themselves, this may be true.

If you are one of these kids, keep appreciating who you are, what you have and the people who have helped you become the kid you are. Be sure to give to others who are less fortunate than you.

If you feel lonely or hate to look at yourself or think of yourself as dumb or feel unloved, you are not alone! It is never too late to remind yourself that you are lovable and worthwhile.

I hope that this book has given you some ideas about how to feel better about yourself. You are each special and important to me. If you want to write to me about a problem you have or if you have an idea about relaxing or getting along better with others or liking yourself better, I'd love to hear from you. I promise I'll write back to you just as soon as I can. Write to me c/o ETR Associates.

Allen Mendler
c/o ETR Associates
P.O. Box 1830
Santa Cruz, CA 95061-1830

Appendix A

Rating Scales

For Parents and Teachers

You can suggest that your child rate him or herself both before and after the activity so that the child can feel some change as a result of the experience. Neither you nor your child should expect major changes as a result of this or any of the activities. The idea is to do stress-reduction/relaxation/appreciation a little every day so that changes which occur gradually have lasting value. You and your child can expand the rating scale to 1-10 (see Fun Rating Scale), which will focus attention on even smaller changes.

Smiling at Yourself Rating Scale ▪▪▪▪▪▪▮▮▮▮▮

Directions: Put a circle around the number on the line that best shows how you feel before doing the smiling activity and then circle the number that shows your feelings after doing the activity. You can use the same scale with many other activities in the book if you like.

Before smiling at myself I felt:

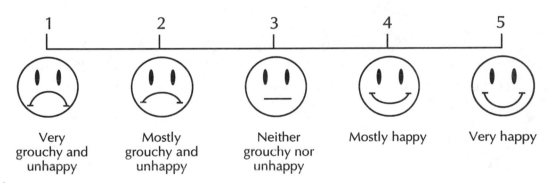

1	2	3	4	5
Very grouchy and unhappy	Mostly grouchy and unhappy	Neither grouchy nor unhappy	Mostly happy	Very happy

After I smiled at myself I felt:

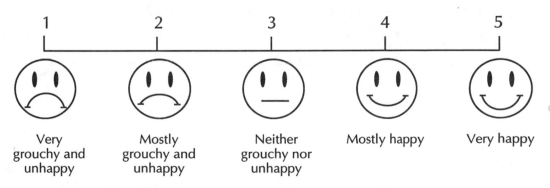

1	2	3	4	5
Very grouchy and unhappy	Mostly grouchy and unhappy	Neither grouchy nor unhappy	Mostly happy	Very happy

Fun Rating Scale ▬▬▬▬▬▬▬▬▬▬▬▬▬▬▬▬▬

Directions: Fill out the rating scale before and after you do the laughing activity.

1. *What were the things you did today that were fun?*
   a.

   b.

   c.

2. *Try to remember how you felt before you did these things today. Circle the number that best shows how you felt.*

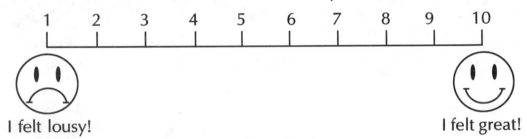

I felt lousy!   I felt great!

3. *How did you feel after you did these fun things?*

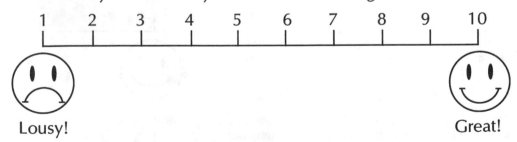

Lousy!   Great!

4. *Did doing fun things make a difference in the way you feel?*

Notebook of Appreciations ▬▬▬▬▬▬▬

Directions: Keep a notebook of things you do or say or feel each day that make you feel proud.

1. Put the date on each page.

2. Write down things (when they happen) that made you feel proud or made you like yourself more. Some examples of things that might be written are:
- ❦ I told my sister when I felt angry instead of saying a bad word.
- ❦ I helped Granny carry in her groceries.
- ❦ I studied hard and did my best.
- ❦ I made myself practice the piano even though it was a beautiful day and I only wanted to play outside.
- ❦ I was offered drugs and I said no!
- ❦ I offered to help a person in a wheelchair get across the street.
- ❦ I read a story to my sister who can't read yet.

3. Keep your own notebook. After a few weeks, you will be able to read back lots of things that you have done which will make you feel really good about yourself.

Relaxing Rating Scale ▪▪▪▪▪▪▪▪▪▪▪▪▪▪▪▪▪▪

1. Circle the number that best tells how you feel *before* you do a relaxation activity.

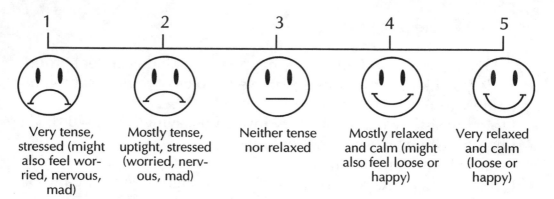

2. Circle the number that best tells how you feel *after* you do a relaxation activity.

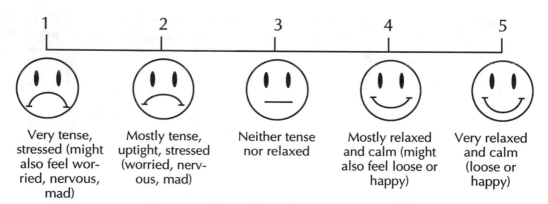

Suggested Readings

Abuse

Lemett, R., and D. Barthlme with B. Crane. *Sometimes it's O.K. to Tell Secrets!—A Parent/Child Manual for the Protection of Children.* New York: Tom Doherty Associates, 1986.

Blended Families

Berman, Clare. *Making It as a Stepparent.* New York: Harper & Row, 1986.

Maddox, Brenda. *The Half Parent.* New York: M. Evans Co., 1975.

Roosevelt, R. and J. Lofas. *Living in Step.* New York: Stein & Day, 1976.

Death

LeShan, Eda. *Learning to Say Goodbye—When a Parent Dies.* New York: Avon Books, 1976.

Schaefer, D. and C. Lyons. *How Do We Tell the Children?—Helping Children Cope and Understand when Someone Dies.* New York: Newmarket Press, 1988.

Schiff, Harriet S. *Living Through Mourning—Finding Comfort and Hope When a Loved One Has Died.* New York: Penguin Books, 1986.

Schmidt, J.S. *How to Cope with Grief.* New York: Ballantine Books, 1989.

Divorce

Gardner, Richard. *The Boys' and Girls' Book About Divorce.* New York: Science House, Inc., 1970.

Grollman, Earl. *Talking About Divorce and Separation—A Dialogue Between Parent and Child.* Boston: Beacon Press, 1975.

Rogers, Fred and Clare O'Brien. *Mister Rogers Talks with Families About Divorce.* New York: Berkeley Publishing Group, 1987.

Drugs and Alcohol

Ackerman, R.L. *Children of Alcoholics.* New York: Simon and Schuster, 1983.

Arterburn, Stephen. *Growing up Addicted.* New York: Random House, 1987.

Baron, J.D. *Kids & Drugs—A Parent's Handbook of Drug Abuse Prevention & Treatment.* New York: Perigree Books, 1983.

Mumey, Jack. *Young Alcoholics—A Book for Parents.* Chicago: Contemporary Books Inc., 1984.

Sunshine, L. and J.W. Wright. *The 100 Best Treatment Centers for Alcoholism and Drug Abuse.* New York: Avon Books, 1988.

Illness/Disability

Cox-Gedmark, Jan. *Coping with Physical Disability.* Philadelphia: The Westminster Press, 1980.

Golant, Mitch with Bob Crane. *It's O.K. to be Different.* New York: Tom Doherty Associates. 1988.

Simons, Robin. *After the Tears—Parents Talk About Raising a Child with a Disability.* New York: Harcourt, Brace, Jovanovich, Inc. 1988.

Stearns, Ann Kaiser. *Coming Back: Rebuilding Lives After Crisis and Loss.* New York: Ballantine Books, 1989.

Other Books About Stress and Self-Esteem

Alberti, R.F. and M.L. Emmons. *Your Perfect Right—A Guide to Assertive Behavior.* San Luis Obispo, CA: Impact Publishers, 1978.

Clark, Jean. *Self-Esteem: A Family Affair.* New York: Harper & Row, 1978.

Curran, Dolores. *Stress and the Healthy Family.* New York: Harper & Row, 1985.

Gerard, P.C. with M. Cohn. *Teaching Your Child Basic Body Confidence.* Boston: Houghton Mifflin, 1988.

Hendricks, G. and T.B. Roberts. *The Self-Centering Book—More Awareness Activities for Children, Parents, and Teachers.* Englewood Cliffs, NJ: Prentice-Hall Inc., 1977.

Kravette, Steve. *Complete Relaxation.* Rockport, MA: Para Research Inc., 1979.

McElroy, Evelyn. *Children and Adolescents with Mental Illness.*

Kensington, MD: Woodbine House, 1987.

Mason, John L. *Stress Passages.* Berkeley, CA: Celestial Arts, 1988.

Tubesing, Donald A. *Kicking Your Stress Habits.* New York: New American Library, 1981.

Wells, Joel. *Coping in the 80's—Eliminating Needless Stress and Guilt.* Chicago: The Thomas More Press, 1986.

Resources on Sensitive Issues for Educators of Young Children

Smiling at Yourself: Educating Young Children About Stress and Self-Esteem
ISBN 0-941816-90-7
150 pages, paperback $14.95

"Does AIDS Hurt?"
Educating Young Children About AIDS
ISBN 0-941816-52-4
149 pages, paperback $14.95

TO ORDER, CALL TOLL-FREE 1 (800) 321-4407 OR RETURN THIS ORDER FORM

TITLE #	TITLE	QTY	CODE	UNIT PRICES	TOTAL
353	"Does AIDS Hurt?"		HURT	$14.95	
506	Smiling At Yourself		YOUR	$14.95	

ORDER SUBTOTAL: $ _____

California Residents add 6% sales tax: +$ _____

Shipping and Handling Charges: +$ _____
(Please add appropriate % from list below):
$10.00-$199.00: Add 15% shipping/handling
$200.00-$499.00: Add 10% shipping/handling
$500.00 and over: Add 8% shipping/handling
All Foreign Orders: Add 15% shipping/handling

TOTAL ORDER COST ($10.00 minimum): $ _____

Please photocopy this order form and mail to:

ETR Associates/Network Publications
P.O. Box 1830
Santa Cruz, CA 95061-1830

Or telephone toll-free 1 (800) 321-4407 between
8:30 a.m. and 5:00 p.m. PST.
FAX (408) 438-4284
Business offices: (408) 438-4060

YOUR GUARANTEE: We guarantee your full satisfaction with all materials produced or distributed by Network Publications. If you are not completely satisfied with any purchase, please return it to us within 30 days for a full and prompt credit or refund.

Please allow 4-6 weeks for delivery.
Canadian/Foreign orders must be *prepaid in U.S. funds only.*
Prices subject to change.
Terms: Net 30 days. 1.5% per month charged after 30 days.

☐ Payment enclosed. (Please make checks payable to: ETR Associates; do not send cash)

☐ Bill me. Purchase Order #_____

Charge to: ☐ VISA ☐ MasterCard

Card Expires
month   year

Account number (include all digits)

Signature _____

Phone (_____) _____
area code
(You must include your signature and phone number with credit card orders.)

Billing Address: Name_____

Organization _____

Address _____

City_____

State/Zip _____

Ordered by _____

Phone (_____) _____
area code

Shipping Address (if different):

Name_____

Organization _____

Address _____

City_____

State/Zip _____

FOR OFFICE USE ONLY	AMT DUE	
ACCT.#	CREDIT DUE	
INV.#		
B/O	SOURCE	_ _ Q7